Third Grade Math
with Confidence

Student Workbook
Part A

Third Grade Math with Confidence

Student Workbook Part A

KATE SNOW

WELL-TRAINED MIND PRESS

Names: Snow, Kate (Teacher), author.

Title: Third grade math with confidence. Student workbook part A / Kate Snow.

Other titles: Student workbook part A

Description: [Charles City, Virginia] : Well-Trained Mind Press, [2023] | Series: Math with confidence | Interest age level: 007-009.

Identifiers: ISBN: 978-1-944481-30-8 (paperback)

Subjects: LCSH: Mathematics--Study and teaching (Elementary) | LCGFT: Problems and exercises. | BISAC: JUVENILE NONFICTION / MATHEMATICS / Arithmetic.

Classification: LCC: QA107.2 .S663 2023 | DDC: 372.7--dc23

Reprinted March 2025 by Versa Press, Inc.

Job #J25-01882

Table of Contents

Author's Note

You'll need three books to teach *Third Grade Math with Confidence*. All three books are essential for the program.

- The Instructor Guide contains the scripted lesson plans for the entire year (Units 1-16).
- Student Workbook Part A contains the workbook pages for the first half of the year (Units 1-8).
- Student Workbook Part B contains the workbook pages for the second half of the year (Units 9-16).

The Student Workbooks are not meant to be used as stand-alone workbooks. The hands-on teaching activities in the Instructor Guide are an essential part of the program. You'll need the directions in the Instructor Guide to guide your child through the Lesson Activities pages. The icon with two heads means that your child should complete these pages with you, and that she is not expected to complete these pages on her own.

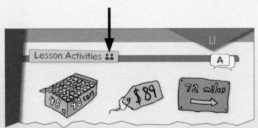

The Practice and Review pages give your child practice with new concepts and review previously-learned skills. The icon with one head means that your child may complete these pages on his own. Most third-graders will be able to complete these workbook pages independently, but some may need help reading and interpreting the directions.

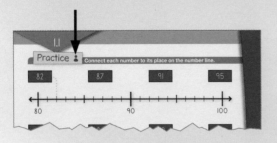 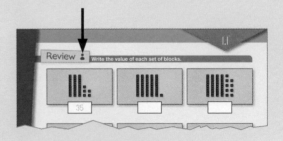

Lesson Activities

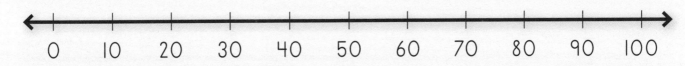

62	69	87	23	18	51	45	96

Round to the Nearest Ten Crash

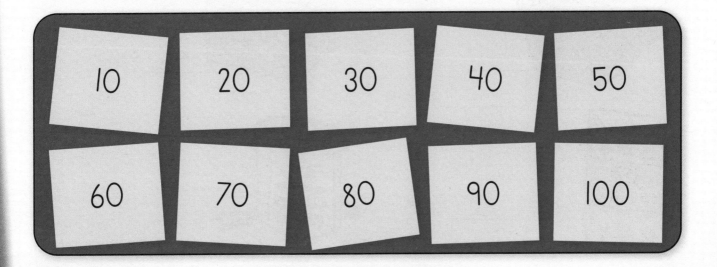

Practice 👤 Connect each number to its place on the number line.

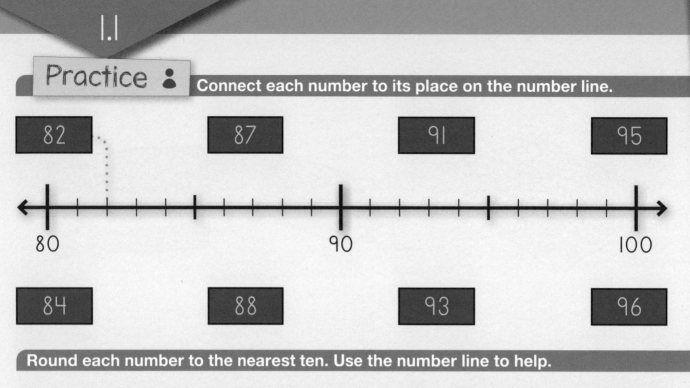

| 82 | 87 | 91 | 95 |

| 84 | 88 | 93 | 96 |

Round each number to the nearest ten. Use the number line to help.

82	91	88	95	93	84	96	87

Round each number to the nearest ten.

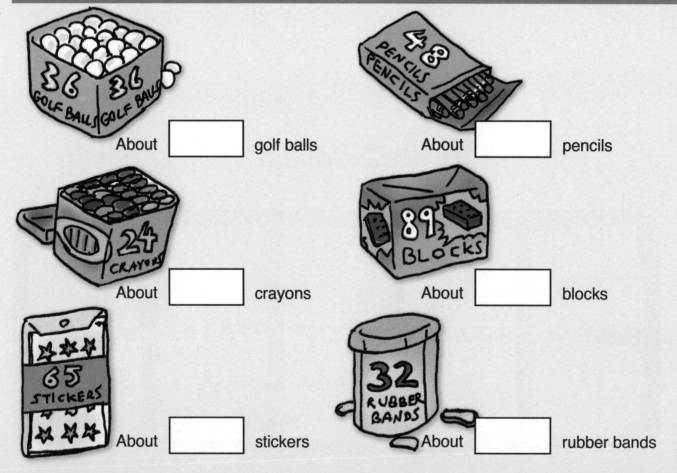

About [ ] golf balls

About [ ] pencils

About [ ] crayons

About [ ] blocks

About [ ] stickers

About [ ] rubber bands

Review 👤 Write the value of each set of blocks.

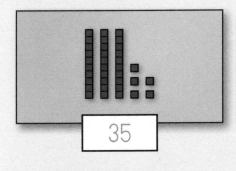

35

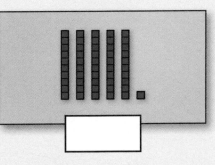

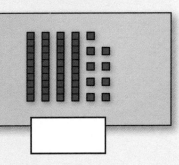

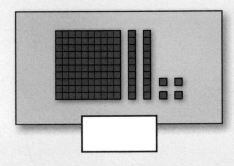

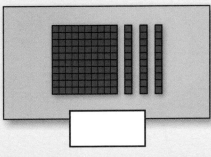

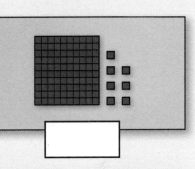

Connect each number to its place on the number line.

| 91 | 97 | 103 | 108 |

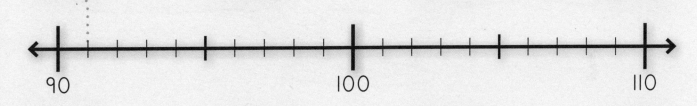

90   100   110

| 94 | 99 | 101 | 105 |

Complete.

-9	
11	2
15	
17	
12	

-8	
16	
10	
14	
17	

-7	
14	
12	
16	
13	

Lesson Activities

87 > 42	42 < 87	42 = 42
↑ greater-than sign	↑ less-than sign	↑ equals sign

60 ◯ 100   38 ◯ 38   49 ◯ 47

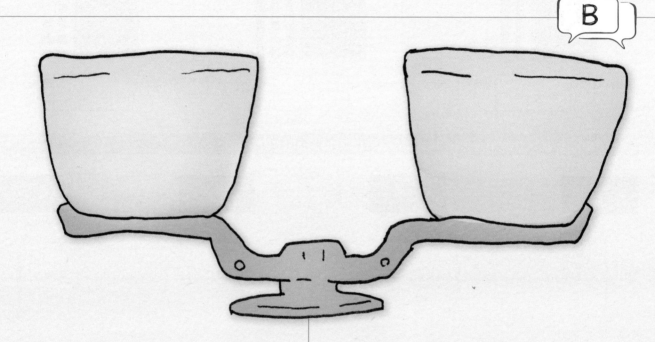

5 ◯ 4   3 + 3 ◯ 7

5 ◯ 8 – 3   6 – 4 ◯ 3

10 ◯ 5 + 4   9 – 1 ◯ 2 + 6

Practice 👤 Complete the circles with <, >, or =.

30 ◯ 40

126 ◯ 26

199 ◯ 201

10 ◯ 9+6

15-5 ◯ 10

10 ◯ 6+4

20+20 ◯ 40

10+30 ◯ 50

60 ◯ 50+9

100 ◯ 30+30

50+50 ◯ 100

100 ◯ 80+40

Write a number in the blank that makes the statement true.

7+6 < ▢

▢ > 7+9

⭐ 7+7 = 9+ ▢

8+8 > ▢

▢ < 12-6

⭐ 12-6 > 11- ▢

9+5 = ▢

▢ > 6+5

⭐ 5+8 < 20- ▢

Review 👤 Complete.

	+5
4	9
7	
8	
6	

	+7
7	
9	
6	
8	

	+6
5	
8	
9	
6	

Connect each number to its place on the number line.

455	458	461	465	466

450   460   470

453	457	459	464	468

Match pairs that equal 100.

90	80
20	25
70	10
75	30
40	99
1	60

Copy the shapes.

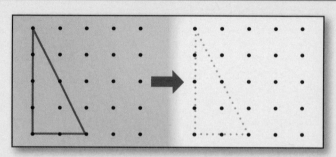

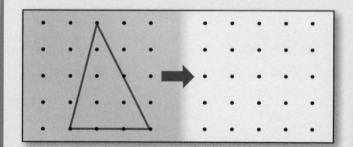

Lesson Activities 👥

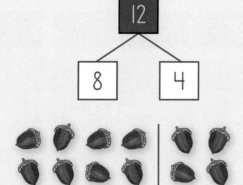

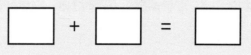

□ + □ = □

□ + □ = □

□ − □ = □

□ − □ = □

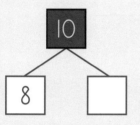

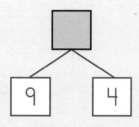

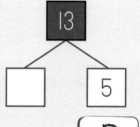

B

□ + 6 = 13

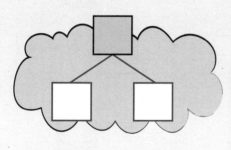

12 − □ = 9

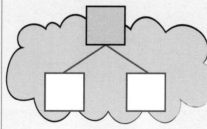

□ − 8 = 7

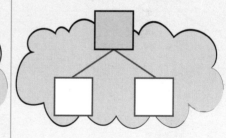

□ + □ = □

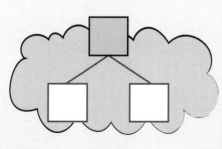

□ − □ = □

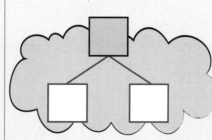

□ − □ = □

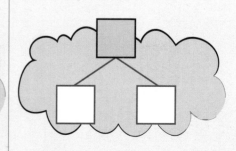

Practice

Use the numbers to complete the blanks.
You will use each number once.

| 0 | 1 | 2 | 3 | 4 | 5 | 6 | 7 | 8 |

$8 + \boxed{} = 9$

$14 - 8 = \boxed{}$

$\boxed{} - 2 = 1$

$10 - \boxed{} = 5$

$3 + 1 = \boxed{}$

$\boxed{} - 5 = 3$

$12 + \boxed{} = 14$

$16 - 9 = \boxed{}$

$\boxed{} + 6 = 6$

Complete.

 12 → 6, ☐

15 → 9, ☐

14 → ☐, 7

13 → 9, ☐

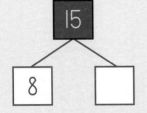 15 → 8, ☐

13 → ☐, 6

16 → ☐, 8

12 → ☐, 3

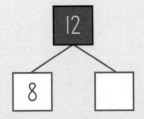 12 → 8, ☐

14 → ☐, 8

13 → 5, ☐

16 → ☐, 7

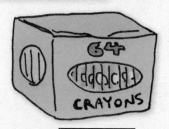

About [   ] crayons

About [   ] stickers

About [   ] packs of crackers

Complete the sequences.

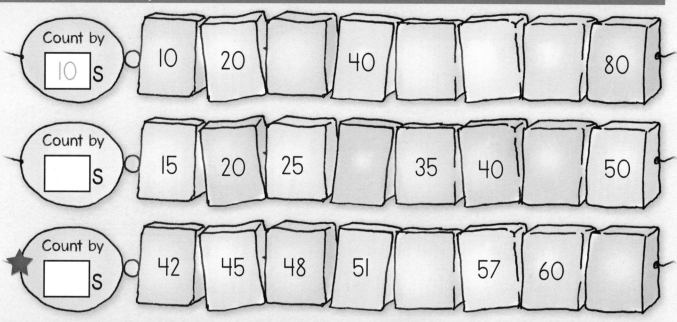

Count by [10]s: 10, 20, ___, 40, ___, ___, ___, 80

Count by [ ]s: 15, 20, 25, ___, 35, 40, ___, 50

Count by [ ]s: ★ 42, 45, 48, 51, ___, 57, 60, ___

Complete.

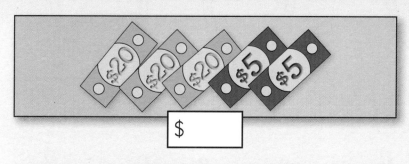

$ [   ]

$ [   ]

Complete.

50 + 40 = [   ]

70 − 20 = [   ]

35 + 10 = [   ]

25 + 25 = [   ]

80 − 40 = [   ]

50 − 20 = [   ]

Lesson Activities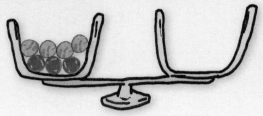

A

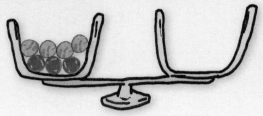

$3 + 4 = \boxed{}$

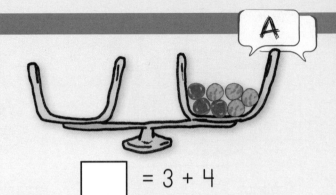

$\boxed{} = 3 + 4$

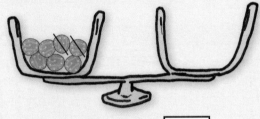

$7 - 2 = \boxed{}$

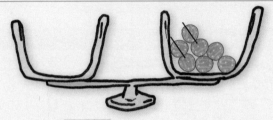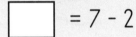

$\boxed{} = 7 - 2$

B

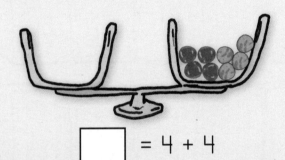

$\boxed{} = 4 + 4$

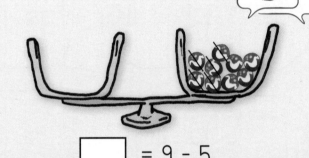

$\boxed{} = 9 - 5$

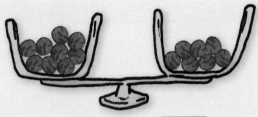

$9 = 7 + \boxed{}$

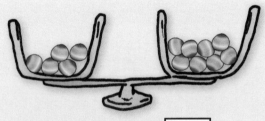

$5 = 8 - \boxed{}$

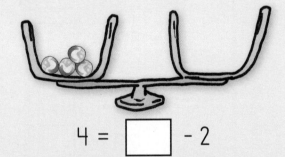

$4 = \boxed{} - 2$

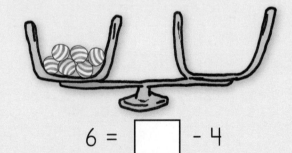

$6 = \boxed{} - 4$

Practice 👤 Complete.

☐ = 8 + 4   ☐ = 7 + 6   ☐ = 4 + 9

☐ = 7 + 8   ☐ = 9 + 9   ☐ = 8 + 5

☐ = 16 - 8   ☐ = 11 - 4   ☐ = 11 - 9

☐ = 14 - 9   ☐ = 13 - 7   ☐ = 15 - 6

Complete. Draw or cross out marbles on the scale to match each completed equation.

10 = 8 + ☐

7 = 9 - ☐

9 = ☐ + 3

6 = 11 - ☐

5 = ☐ - 3

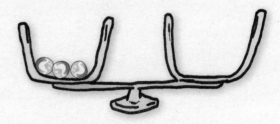

3 = ☐ - 7

Review 👤 Use the graph to complete the chart.

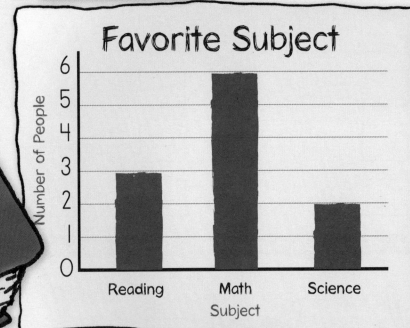

Favorite Subject

Subject	Number of People
Reading	
Math	
Science	

Color the even numbers green. Color the odd numbers blue. | Complete.

26 8 112 80 450 689 647 554 283 395

$$99 + \boxed{} = 100$$

$$98 + \boxed{} = 100$$

$$97 + \boxed{} = 100$$

$$96 + \boxed{} = 100$$

$$95 + \boxed{} = 100$$

Match.

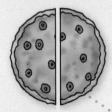   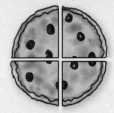 

| Eighths | Halves | Fourths | Sixths | Thirds |

Lesson Activities

How to Read Word Problems

1. Read the problem.

2. Identify the goal.

3. Read the problem again.

   • Read slowly and carefully.
   • Imagine what's happening.
   • Stop after each sentence to make sure you understand it.

4. Solve.

You have $15.
Then, you earn $10 more.
How much money do you have?

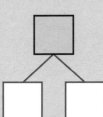

You pay $15 for a book and a
box of markers. The book costs $10.
How much do the markers cost?

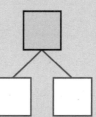

You have 10 inches of red ribbon.
You have 6 inches of blue ribbon.
How many more inches of red ribbon
do you have than blue?

greater number − lesser number = difference

1.5

Practice :bust_in_silhouette: Solve. Write the equations you use.

How much does it cost to buy the squirrel and the teddy bear?

How much more does the whale cost than the snake?

You have $16. Then, you buy the squirrel. How much money do you have left?

How much does it cost to buy 2 monkeys?

How much less does the snake cost than the monkey?

 How much does it cost to buy all 5 stuffed animals?

Review

Match.

600 + 20 + 4	604	900 + 80	908
600 + 4	640	900 + 8	890
600 + 40	624	800 + 9	980
600 + 40 + 2	642	800 + 90	809

Complete with <, >, or =.

25 + 25 ◯ 50

50 ◯ 30 + 30

30 + 30 ◯ 59

40 ◯ 100 - 50

101 - 1 ◯ 60 + 40

Complete.

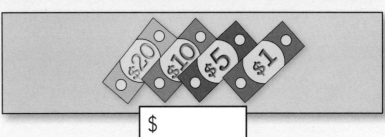

$ [____]

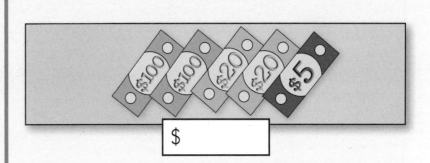

$ [____]

Complete.

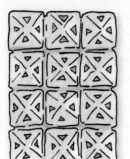
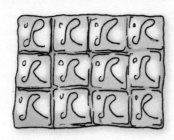

[____] tiles   [____] tiles

Complete.

1 week = [____] days

1 day = [____] hours

1 hour = [____] minutes

1 minute = [____] seconds

Lesson Activities 👥

A

Oscar has $11 to spend at the carnival.
He spends $4 on a snack.
Then, he spends $3 at the arcade.
How much money does he have now?

Arthur has 9 library books.
He takes 6 books back to the library.
Then, he checks out 10 more.
How many library books does he have now?

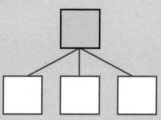

B

The ice cream shop sold 12 ice cream cones.
4 were chocolate.
5 were vanilla.
The rest were strawberry.
How many were strawberry?

Aman spent 30 minutes on all his chores.
He spent 10 minutes washing dishes.
He spent 5 minutes sweeping.
He spent the rest of the time cleaning his room.
How long did he spend cleaning his room?

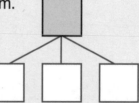

Practice

Solve. Complete the Part-Total diagram to match.

Gabby spends $10 in all at the yard sale.
She spends $4 on a shirt.
She spends $3 on books.
She spends the rest on a board game.
How much does the board game cost?

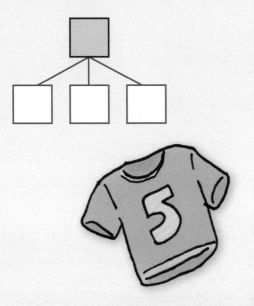

Gavin has 16 googly eyes.
He puts 2 eyes on an octopus.
He puts 8 eyes on a monster.
How many googly eyes does he have left?

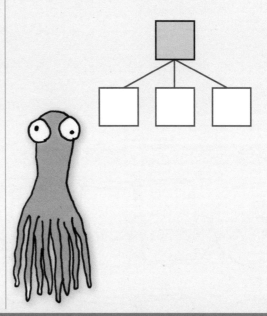

Solve. Write the equations you use.

Connor brought 12 cookies for the bake sale.
Josie brought 6 cookies for the bake sale.
They sold 8 cookies.
How many cookies did they have left?

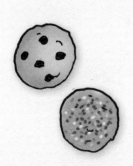

Serena has 10 trading cards.
She gives 4 to her brother.
Then, she buys 9 more.
How many trading cards does she have now?

Review 👤 Draw a shape to match each description.

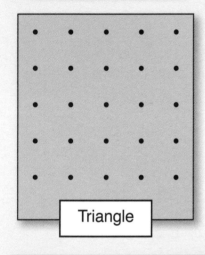

Triangle

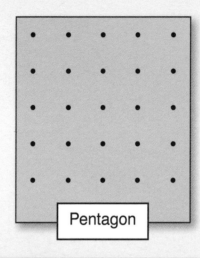

Pentagon

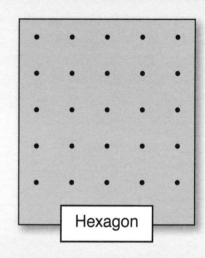

Hexagon

Complete the sequences.

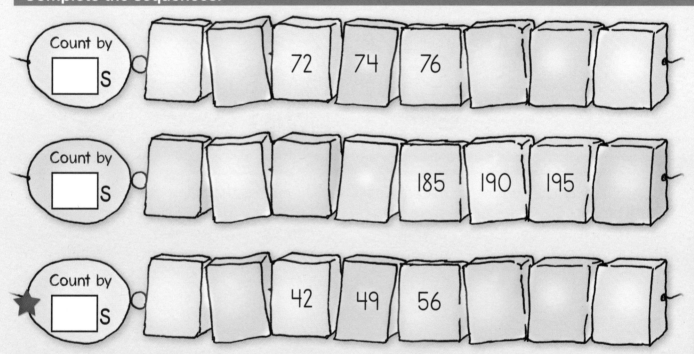

Count by ▢ S   72 74 76

Count by ▢ S   185 190 195

Count by ▢ S   42 49 56

Draw lines to divide each cake into equal parts.

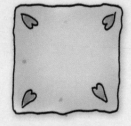

Halves

Fourths

Eighths

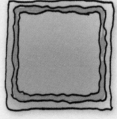

Thirds

Sixths

Lesson Activities

The Addition Algorithm

*** Start with the ones-place.

Add the digits. → Is the sum greater than 9? — YES → Trade. → Record your work. / NO → Record your work.

*** Follow the steps for all the places.

3	9
+ 5	7

2	6
+ 6	8

5	7
+ 5	2

7	6
+ 8	4

Leaf Fight

90 49 28 74 51 83 65 37 92 50

Practice 👤 Complete.

	8	0
+	3	6

	6	3
+	2	4

	4	5
+	2	6

	7	8
+	2	9

Review 👤 Use a ruler to measure in inches.

 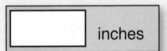 inches

  inches

  inches

Complete.

1 foot = ☐ inches

1 yard = ☐ inches

1 yard = ☐ feet

1 meter = ☐ centimeters

Write a.m. or p.m. for each time.

Storytime 10:15 ☐

Soccer Practice 4:30 ☐

Complete.

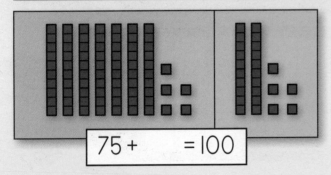

75 + ☐ = 100

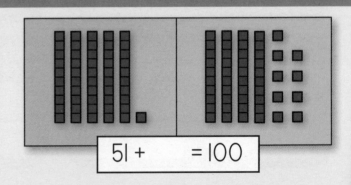

51 + ☐ = 100

Lesson Activities 👥

The Subtraction Algorithm

* * * Start with the ones-place.

Is the top digit greater than or equal to the bottom digit? — YES → Subtract.

NO → Trade. → Subtract.

* * * Follow the steps for all the places.

7	2
− 2	9

9	6
− 5	8

8	0
− 4	7

6	5
− 2	3

Leaf Fight

90 49 28 74 51 83 65 37 92 50

Practice 👤 Complete.

	4	2
−	1	6

	8	0
−	2	7

	8	4
−	3	5

	9	0
−	8	3

Review 👤 Use a ruler to measure in centimeters.

___ centimeters

___ centimeters

___ centimeters

Write the time.

___ : ___

___ : ___

___ : ___

___ : ___

Complete.

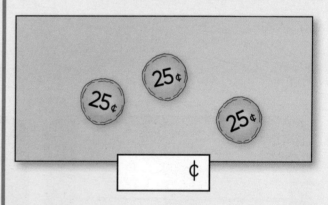

25¢   25¢   25¢   25¢

___ ¢

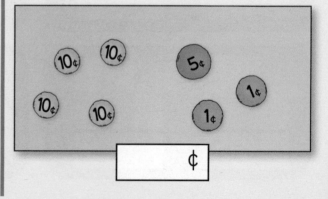

10¢   10¢   5¢   10¢   10¢   1¢   1¢

___ ¢

Lesson Activities 👥

Points Scored in Last Night's Game

Player	Points
Arjun	6
Brynn	10
Claire	3
Dan	7
Eve	4

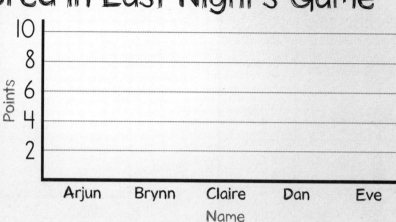

Points Scored This Season

Player	Points
Arjun	20
Brynn	35
Claire	22
Dan	19
Eve	6

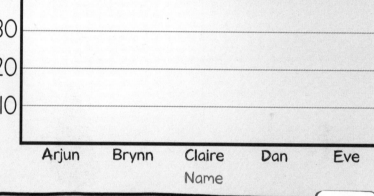

How many more points has Brynn scored than Dan this season?

How many points has the team scored in all this season?

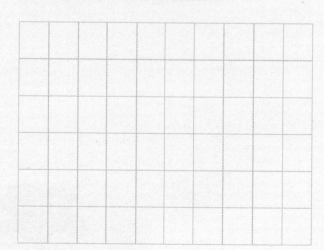

Practice

Use the chart to make a bar graph.

Type of Tree	Number of Trees
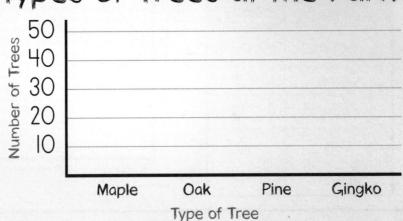 Maple	49
Oak	25
Pine	32
Gingko	17

Types of Trees at the Park

Number of Trees

50
40
30
20
10

Maple   Oak   Pine   Gingko

Type of Tree

Use the chart to solve. Write the equations you use.

How many trees are maples or oaks?

How many more pine trees than gingko trees are there?

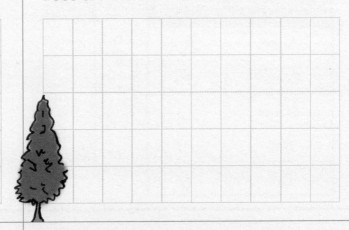

If the park plants 9 more oak trees, how many oak trees will there be?

How many trees are listed in all in the chart?

Review 👤 Use a ruler to draw a line that matches each length.

5 inches

9 centimeters

Complete.

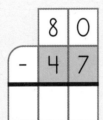

```
  3 7
+ 5 6
─────
```

```
  8 4
+ 1 7
─────
```

```
  9 2
- 3 5
─────
```

```
  8 0
- 4 7
─────
```

Round to the nearest ten.

16	
27	
43	
85	
96	

Write each amount of money two ways.

25¢ 25¢ 25¢

$ ___   ___ ¢

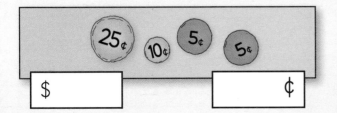

25¢ 10¢ 5¢ 5¢

$ ___   ___ ¢

Write the time.

___ : ___   ___ : ___

Unit Wrap-Up

Complete the fact family to match the Part-Total diagram.

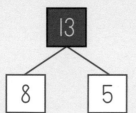

☐ + ☐ = ☐

☐ + ☐ = ☐

☐ - ☐ = ☐

☐ - ☐ = ☐

Match.

The sum of 7 and 4		3
The difference between 7 and 4		11
The sum of 7, 4, and 2		13

Round to the nearest ten.

47	
19	
65	
97	

Complete with <, >, or =.

10 – 7 ◯ 5

10 + 15 ◯ 20

9 ◯ 20 – 10

35 ◯ 20 + 10

Complete.

7 + ☐ = 12   ☐ = 8 + 8   12 = 7 + ☐

10 – ☐ = 7   ☐ = 15 – 6   10 = 14 – ☐

Unit Wrap-Up 👤 Complete.

```
  4 2          8 7          8 5          8 0
+ 3 9        - 3 5        + 4 8        - 4 7
```

Carlos made a chart to show how high the kids in his family can jump. Use the chart to complete the graph.

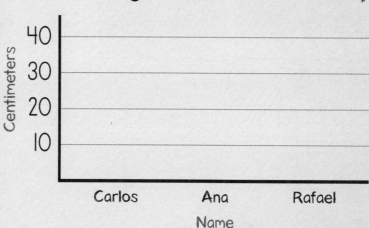

Name	Centimeters
Carlos	25
Ana	34
Rafael	19

How High We Can Jump

Solve. Write the equations you use.

Ana can jump 34 centimeters high. Rafael can jump 19 centimeters high. How much higher can Ana jump than Rafael?

15 birds are sitting in a tree. 6 are red, 5 are brown, and the rest are yellow. How many birds are yellow?

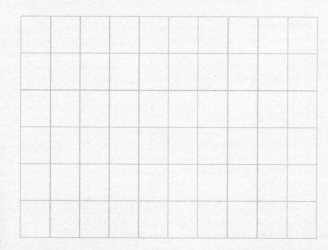

2.1

Lesson Activities 👥

Repeated Addition	Multiplication
3 groups of 4	3 groups of 4
4 + 4 + 4 = ☐	3 × 4 = ☐

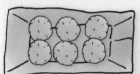 

2 groups of 6

5 groups of 3

☐ + ☐ + ☐ + ☐ + ☐ = ☐

Cookie Order	Multiplication Equation
3 boxes of 6	
4 boxes of 4	
1 box of 8	
2 boxes of 7	
5 boxes of 2	

Practice 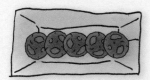 Complete.

 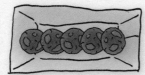

2 groups of 5

$2 \times 5 = \boxed{}$

3 groups of 3

$3 \times 3 = \boxed{}$

4 groups of 2

$\boxed{4} \times \boxed{2} = \boxed{}$

4 groups of 4

$\boxed{} \times \boxed{} = \boxed{}$

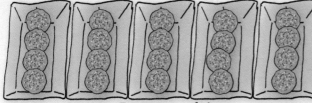

5 groups of 4

$\boxed{} \times \boxed{} = \boxed{}$

4 groups of 5

$\boxed{} \times \boxed{} = \boxed{}$

5 groups of 1

$\boxed{} \times \boxed{} = \boxed{}$

5 groups of 0

$\boxed{} \times \boxed{} = \boxed{}$

1 group of 9

$\boxed{} \times \boxed{} = \boxed{}$

   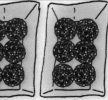

4 groups of 6

$\boxed{} \times \boxed{} = \boxed{}$

Review 🧍 Complete.

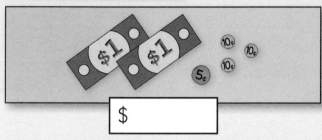

$ [ ]

$ [ ]

Complete.

	Double
10	20
11	
40	
42	
45	
50	

Write the value of the base-ten blocks.

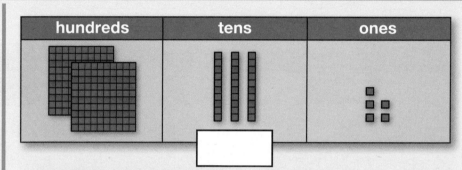

hundreds	tens	ones
	[ ]	

hundreds	tens	ones
	[ ]	

Complete.

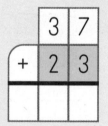

	3	7
+	2	3

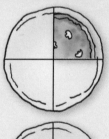

	8	0
−	4	7

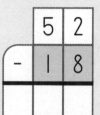

	5	2
−	1	8

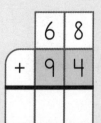

	6	8
+	9	4

Match.

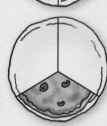

$\frac{1}{8}$

$\frac{1}{3}$

$\frac{1}{4}$

Lesson Activities 👥

A

3 groups of 5

 × ☐ = ☐

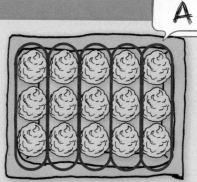

5 groups of 3

 × = ☐

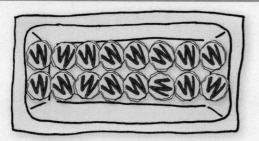

☐ × = ☐

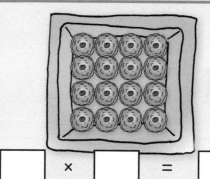

☐ × ☐ = ☐

B

Order (Rows x Columns)	Total Squares
3 × 3	
7 × 2	
1 × 6	
5 × 5	
3 × 8	

Practice 👤 Write an equation to match each array.

☐ × ☐ = ☐   ☐ × ☐ = ☐

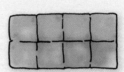

☐ × ☐ = ☐   ☐ × ☐ = ☐

Draw an array to match each equation. Then, complete the equation.

2 × 6 = ☐

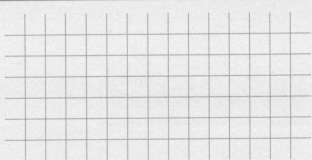

4 × 5 = ☐

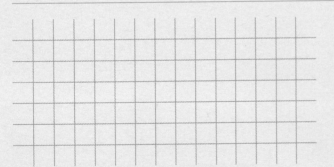

5 × 6 = ☐

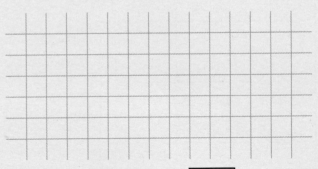

3 × 7 = ☐

Review 👤 Complete.

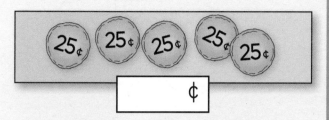

_____ ¢

_____ ¢

Write the time.

_____ : _____   _____ : _____

Write a.m. or p.m. for each time.

Breakfast 7:30 [ ]

Lunch 12:30 [ ]

Dinner 6:00 [ ]

Solve.

Greyson helped his mom plant 50 flower bulbs.
32 were tulips.
The rest were daffodils.
How many were daffodils?

Match.

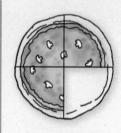

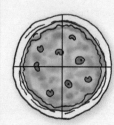

2.3

 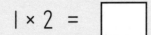
1 × 2 = ☐   6 × 2 = ☐

2 × 2 = ☐   7 × 2 = ☐

3 × 2 = ☐   8 × 2 = ☐

4 × 2 = ☐   9 × 2 = ☐

5 × 2 = ☐   10 × 2 = ☐

B

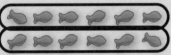

2 groups of 6

2 × 6 = ☐

6 groups of 2

6 × 2 = ☐

10 × 2 = ☐   8 × 2 = ☐   9 × 2 = ☐

2 × 10 = ☐   2 × 8 = ☐   2 × 9 = ☐

C

Multiplication Crash (×2)

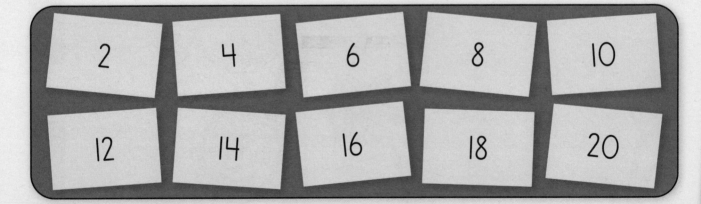

Practice 👤 Complete.

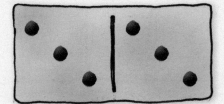

2 × 3 = ☐

2 × 5 = ☐

2 × 8 = ☐

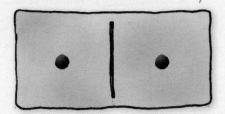

2 × 1 = ☐

2 × 7 = ☐

2 × 6 = ☐

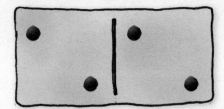

2 × 2 = ☐

2 × 9 = ☐

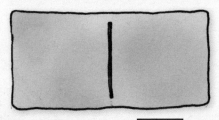

2 × 0 = ☐

2 × 4 = ☐

Review 👤 Complete the sequences.

Count by 1s: 317 | 318 | | | | | | 324

Count by 2s: 540 | 542 | | | | | | 554

Count by 5s: 900 | 905 | | | | | 930 |

Complete.

$3 + 4 =$ ☐

$30 + 40 =$ ☐

$300 + 400 =$ ☐

$8 - 2 =$ ☐

$80 - 20 =$ ☐

$800 - 200 =$ ☐

$6 +$ ☐ $= 10$

$60 +$ ☐ $= 100$

$600 +$ ☐ $= 1,000$

Complete.

$

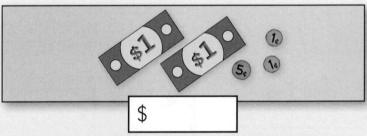

$

Solve.

Tia practiced violin for 15 minutes on Monday, 30 minutes on Tuesday, and 25 minutes on Wednesday. How many minutes did she practice?

Multiplication Bingo (×2)

B	I	N	G	O
2	8	20	14	18
10	20	16	6	4
16	14	12	10	18
8	2	18	20	16
14	6	4	4	12

B	I	N	G	O
12	10	6	20	4
18	6	2	14	8
16	8	10	4	12
20	4	14	8	18
16	2	10	6	2

B

3 × 1 = ☐　　　　　　1 × 3 = ☐

6 × 1 = ☐　　　　1 × 7 = ☐　　　　250 × 1 = ☐

C

3 × 0 = ☐　　　　　0 × 3 = ☐

6 × 0 = ☐　　　　0 × 7 = ☐　　　　250 × 0 = ☐

Practice 👤 Match.

| 1 × 2 | | 2 × 2 |

| | 0 | |

| 2 × 3 | | 1 × 8 |

| | 2 | |

| 6 × 0 | | 10 × 0 |

| | 4 | |

| 10 × 1 | | 2 × 5 |

| | 6 | |

| 4 × 2 | | 2 × 1 |

| | 8 | |

| | 10 | |

| 4 × 1 | | 6 × 1 |

Complete.

$2 \times 10 = \boxed{}$ $1 \times 5 = \boxed{}$ $6 \times 2 = \boxed{}$

$9 \times 0 = \boxed{}$ $2 \times 9 = \boxed{}$ $1 \times 8 = \boxed{}$

$8 \times 2 = \boxed{}$ $2 \times 5 = \boxed{}$ $7 \times 2 = \boxed{}$

⭐ $1 \times 396 = \boxed{}$ ⭐ $37 \times 0 = \boxed{}$ ⭐ $0 \times 200 = \boxed{}$

Review — Complete the sequences.

Count by 100s: 200, ___, 400, ___, ___, ___, ___, 900

Count by 50s: 250, 300, 350, ___, 450, ___, ___, 600

Count by 10s: 570, ___, 590, ___, 610, ___, ___, 640

Copy the shapes.

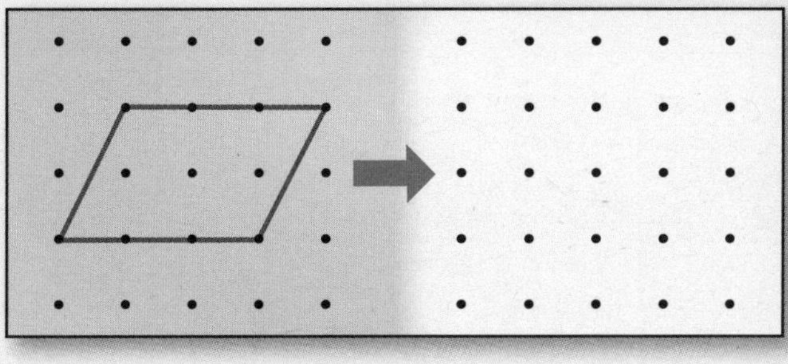

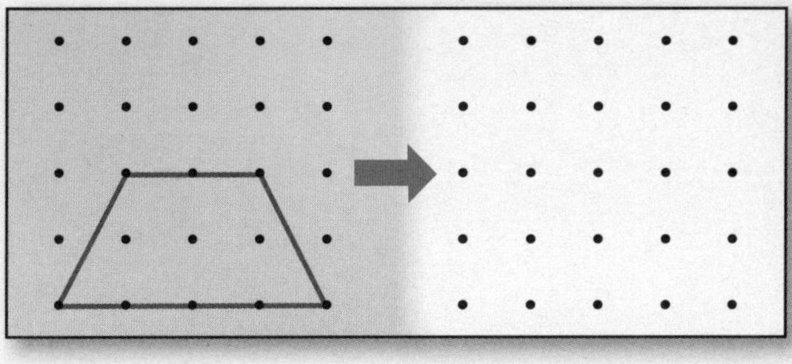

Complete.

```
    7 8
  + 6 2
  _____
```

```
    7 6
  - 2 9
  _____
```

Solve.

Luna had $53. Then, she spent $27.
How much did she have left?

Complete with <, >, or =.

600 ◯ 500

2 ◯ 200

301 ◯ 300

301 ◯ 301

Lesson Activities

$4 \times 10 =$ ☐

$4_{\text{tens}} =$ ☐

$6 \times 10 =$ ☐ $9 \times 10 =$ ☐ $8 \times 10 =$ ☐

$3 \times 10 =$ ☐ $7 \times 10 =$ ☐ $10 \times 10 =$ ☐

Tic-Tac-Toe Crash (×10)

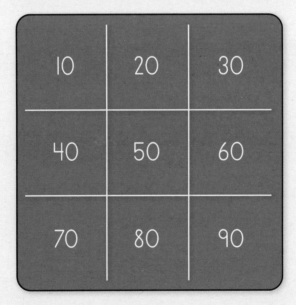

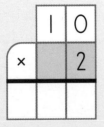 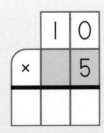 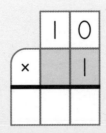

Practice Complete.

3 × 10 = ☐

5 × 10 = ☐

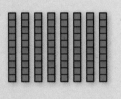

8 × 10 = ☐

6 × 10 = ☐

4 × 10 = ☐

2 × 10 = ☐

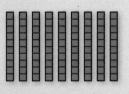

9 × 10 = ☐

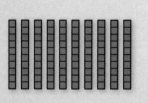

10 × 10 = ☐

 14 × 10 = ☐   30 × 10 = ☐

Review 👤 Complete.

☐ = 7 + 8   10 = 14 − ☐   5 = ☐ − 4

☐ = 12 − 3   17 = 12 + ☐   2 = ☐ − 9

☐ = 9 + 9   3 = 8 − ☐   8 = ☐ − 5

Complete.
Round each number to the nearest ten.

9	43	72	58	65	36	99	22

Match.

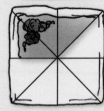

$\dfrac{3}{6}$

$\dfrac{3}{3}$

$\dfrac{3}{4}$

$\dfrac{3}{8}$

Complete with <, >, or =.

40 + 20 ◯ 70

100 ◯ 50 + 50

86 − 6 ◯ 70 + 4

11 ◯ 20 − 7

36 + 42 ◯ 36 + 43

100 − 37 ◯ 100 − 82

Lesson Activities

$$9 \times 2 = 18$$

factors   product

Shopping List

☐ packs of scissors

☐ × ☐ = ☐

☐ packs of pencils

☐ × ☐ = ☐

☐ boxes of markers

☐ × ☐ = ☐

☐ packs of staplers

☐ × ☐ = ☐

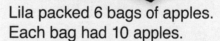

Julius has 2 bags of erasers.
Each bag has 8 erasers.
How many erasers does he have in all?

Lila packed 6 bags of apples.
Each bag had 10 apples.
How many apples did she pack in all?

Practice Complete.

| 1 0 |
| × 3 |

| 1 0 |
| × 7 |

| 1 0 |
| × 5 |

| 1 0 |
| × 2 |

| 1 0 |
| × 8 |

| 1 0 |
| × 4 |

| 1 0 |
| × 1 0 |

| 1 0 |
| × 1 |

| 1 0 |
| × 9 |

| 1 0 |
| × 6 |

| 2 |
| × 7 |

| 6 |
| × 0 |

| 2 |
| × 9 |

| 8 |
| × 2 |

| 1 |
| × 5 |

Solve. Write a multiplication equation to match.

Lucas drew 4 robots.
He drew 3 heads on each robot.
How many heads did he draw?

☐ × ☐ = ☐

Kali drew 5 cacti.
She drew 2 arms on each cactus.
How many arms did she draw?

☐ × ☐ = ☐

Review 👤 Complete.

Count by 100s: 600 ___ 1,000

Count by 50s: 700 750

Count by 10s: 900 910

Complete.

```
  4 7
+ 9 3
-----
```

```
  8 4
- 4 9
-----
```

Write the time.

Use a ruler to measure in centimeters.

centimeters

centimeters

2.7

 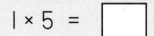
A

1 × 5 = ☐   6 × 5 = ☐

2 × 5 = ☐   7 × 5 = ☐

3 × 5 = ☐   8 × 5 = ☐

4 × 5 = ☐   9 × 5 = ☐

5 × 5 = ☐   10 × 5 = ☐

B

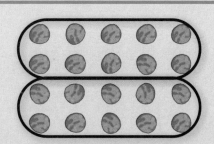

4 × 5 = ☐

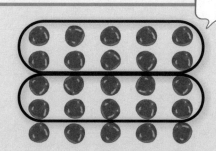

5 × 5 = ☐

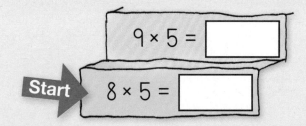

9 × 5 = ☐

8 × 5 = ☐

Start

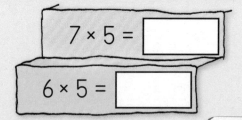

7 × 5 = ☐

6 × 5 = ☐

C

Multiplication Cover Up

Player 1	5	10	15	20	25	30	35	40	45	50
Player 2	5	10	15	20	25	30	35	40	45	50

Practice 👤 Draw a circle around groups of $10. Then, complete.

4 × 5 = ☐

5 × 5 = ☐

2 × 5 = ☐

3 × 5 = ☐

8 × 5 = ☐

9 × 5 = ☐

6 × 5 = ☐

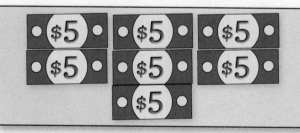

7 × 5 = ☐

★ 20 × 5 = ☐   ★ 21 × 5 = ☐

Review

Solve. Write the equations you use.

Naomi has $11.
She earns $3 for helping in the garden.
Then, she spends $6 at the toy store.
How much money does she have left?

Sam brought 48 cupcakes to the bake sale.
Xander brought 36 cupcakes to the bake sale.
How many more cupcakes did Sam bring than Xander?

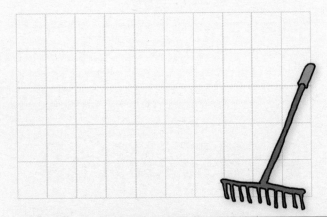

Complete.

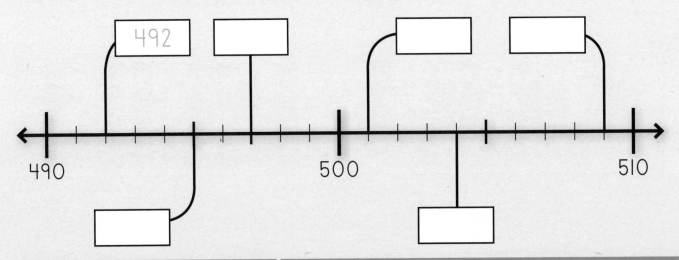

492

490   500   510

Complete.

1 foot = ☐ inches

1 yard = ☐ feet

1 yard = ☐ inches

1 meter = ☐ centimeters

Complete.

$7 \times 2 =$ ☐ $6 \times 10 =$ ☐

$10 \times 9 =$ ☐ $2 \times 8 =$ ☐

$5 \times 10 =$ ☐ $6 \times 2 =$ ☐

$9 \times 2 =$ ☐ $10 \times 8 =$ ☐

Lesson Activities

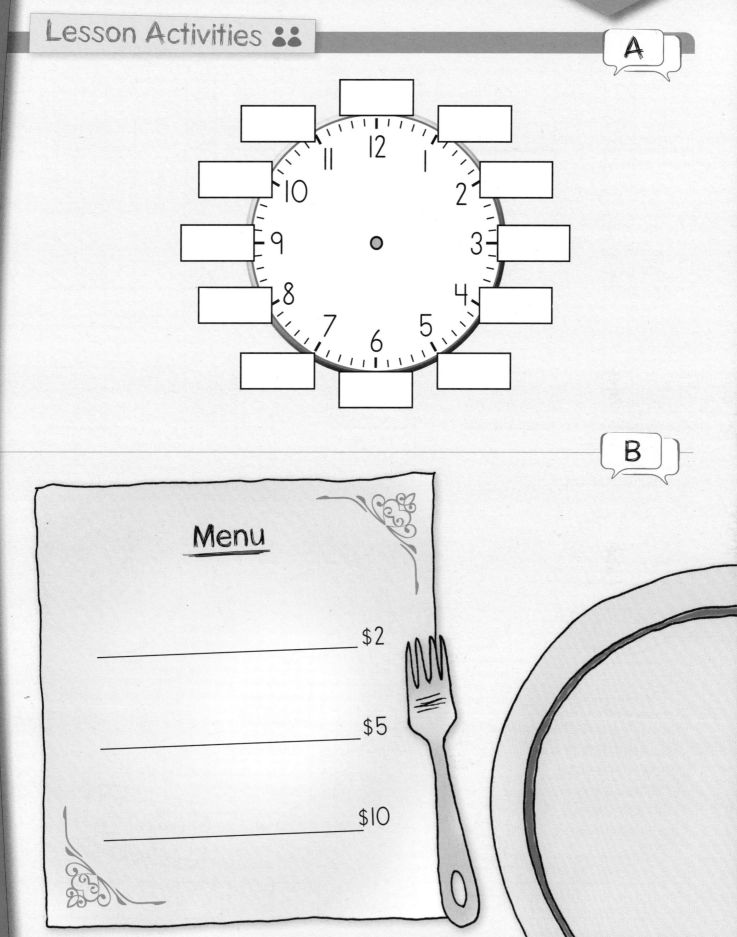

Practice 👤 Complete.

$$\times \begin{array}{c} 3 \\ 5 \end{array} \qquad \times \begin{array}{c} 5 \\ 5 \end{array} \qquad \times \begin{array}{c} 6 \\ 5 \end{array} \qquad \times \begin{array}{c} 2 \\ 5 \end{array} \qquad \times \begin{array}{c} 8 \\ 5 \end{array}$$

$$\times \begin{array}{c} 1 \\ 5 \end{array} \qquad \times \begin{array}{c} 9 \\ 5 \end{array} \qquad \times \begin{array}{c} 4 \\ 5 \end{array} \qquad \times \begin{array}{c} 7 \\ 5 \end{array} \qquad \times \begin{array}{c} 10 \\ 5 \end{array}$$

$$\times \begin{array}{c} 10 \\ 9 \end{array} \qquad \times \begin{array}{c} 8 \\ 2 \end{array} \qquad \times \begin{array}{c} 10 \\ 6 \end{array} \qquad \times \begin{array}{c} 1 \\ 7 \end{array} \qquad \times \begin{array}{c} 9 \\ 2 \end{array}$$

Write the time.

 :  : 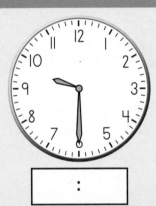 :  :

Solve. Write a multiplication problem to match.

Simon put 5 pieces of candy in each bag. He filled 6 bags. How many pieces of candy did he use?

☐ × ☐ = ☐

Each movie ticket costs $10. How much does it cost to buy 6 movie tickets?

☐ × ☐ = ☐

Review

Complete.

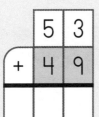

```
  5 3
+ 4 9
─────
```

```
  5 3
- 4 9
─────
```

Match.

700 + 2	720
700 + 20 + 8	702
700 + 20	782
700 + 8	728
700 + 80	708
700 + 80 + 2	780

Kai made a chart to show the height of the kids in his family. Use the chart to complete the graph and answer the questions.

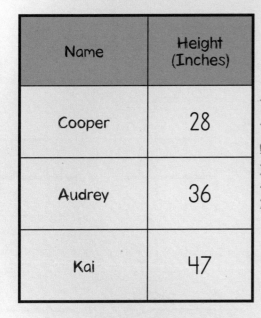

Name	Height (Inches)
Cooper	28
Audrey	36
Kai	47

Our Heights

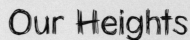
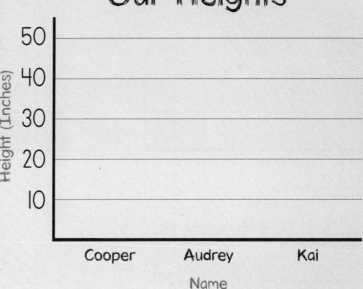

How much taller is Kai than Cooper?

How much shorter is Audrey than Kai?

Unit Wrap-Up 👤   Write an equation to match each array.

[ ] × [ ] = [ ]   [ ] × [ ] = [ ]

Draw an array to match each equation. Then, complete the equation.

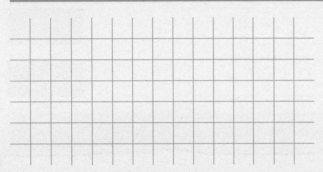   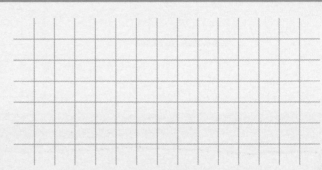

2 × 7 = [ ]   5 × 8 = [ ]

Complete.

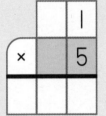

| × | 1 5 | | × | 2 8 | | × | 10 7 | | × | 6 2 | | × | 7 5 |

| × | 10 6 | | × | 10 9 | | × | 7 2 | | × | 3 5 | | × | 4 0 |

| × | 5 5 | | × | 9 2 | | × | 10 8 | | × | 9 5 | | × | 10 0 |

Unit Wrap-Up 👤 Match.

6 × 5		2 × 10
4 × 5	10	4 × 10
10 × 5	20	1 × 10
2 × 5	30	5 × 10
8 × 5	40	3 × 10
	50	

Use the chart to answer the questions.
Write a multiplication equation for each question.

How much do 4 drinks cost?

☐ × ☐ = $ ☐

How much do 8 drinks cost?

☐ × ☐ = $ ☐

MENU

Drink $2

Nachos.............. $5

Taco Plate $10

How much do 6 orders of nachos cost?

☐ × ☐ = $ ☐

How much do 3 taco plates cost?

☐ × ☐ = $ ☐

How much do 9 orders of nachos cost?

☐ × ☐ = $ ☐

How much do 7 taco plates cost?

☐ × ☐ = $ ☐

Lesson Activities

A

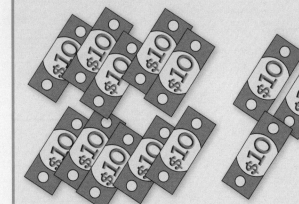

13 tens = ☐

10 tens = ☐
3 tens = ☐

12 tens = ☐   18 tens = ☐   20 tens = ☐

B

70 + 50 = ☐

7 tens + 5 tens = ☐ tens

70 + 63 = ☐   85 + 42 = ☐

70 + 53 = ☐   85 + 40 = ☐

Start 70 + 50 = ☐   80 + 40 = ☐

Four in a Row

160	60+90	70+60	120	80+60
120	90+70	150	80+80	160
80+50	140	70+70	90+50	80+90
140	90+30	130	90+90	150
70+80	180	130	70+50	170

Practice

Color the problems that equal the number in the star.

100	110	120	130
50 + 50	60 + 50	90 + 40	70 + 60
10 + 90	40 + 70	60 + 60	30 + 90
40 + 60	20 + 90	30 + 80	50 + 80
70 + 40	30 + 80	50 + 70	50 + 60
80 + 30	50 + 70	40 + 80	90 + 40

3.1

Review

Connect each number to its place on the number line.

392	395	401	407

390   400   410

396	398	404	409

Solve.

Serena has 40 trading cards.
She buys 10 more.
Then, she gives 20 to her brother.
How many trading cards does she have now?

Match.

$\dfrac{3}{4}$

$\dfrac{5}{8}$

$\dfrac{2}{3}$

$\dfrac{5}{6}$

Complete.

		5
×		6

		8
×		2

		2
×		6

		5
×		9

	1	0
×	1	0

	1	0
×		2

		5
×		7

	1	0
×		4

		9
×		2

		5
×		8

Lesson Activities

 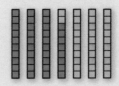 

38 + ☐ = 40   38 + ☐ = 70   38 + ☐ = 100

49 + ☐ = 50   67 + ☐ = 70   52 + ☐ = 80

76 + ☐ = 90   85 + ☐ = 100   27 + ☐ = 100

Pretend Store

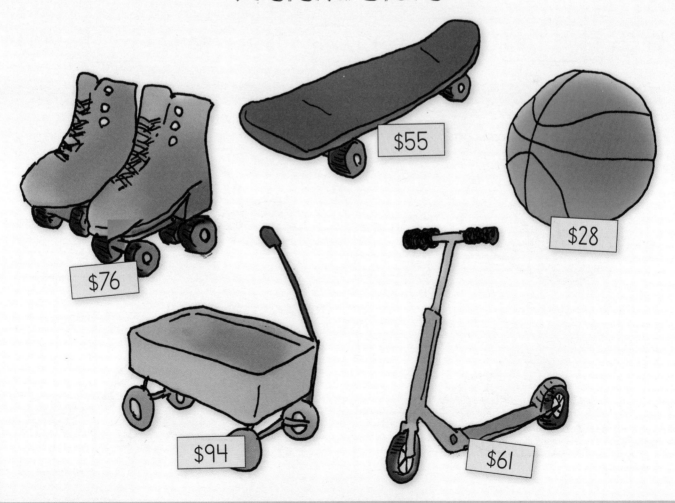

$55

$28

$76

$94

$61

Practice 👤 Complete.

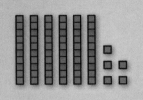

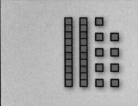

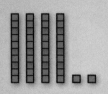

$65 + \boxed{} = 70$

$65 + \boxed{} = 80$

$65 + \boxed{} = 90$

$65 + \boxed{} = 100$

⭐ $65 + \boxed{} = 110$

$29 + \boxed{} = 30$

$29 + \boxed{} = 40$

$29 + \boxed{} = 70$

$29 + \boxed{} = 100$

⭐ $29 + \boxed{} = 130$

$42 + \boxed{} = 50$

$42 + \boxed{} = 70$

$42 + \boxed{} = 80$

$42 + \boxed{} = 100$

⭐ $42 + \boxed{} = 200$

Solve.

You pay the clerk $20.
How much change do you get?

$19

Change
$

You pay the clerk $60.
How much change do you get?

$48

Change
$

You pay the clerk $80.
How much change do you get?

$71

Change
$

You pay the clerk $100.
How much change do you get?

$36

Change
$

Review Complete the sequences.

Count by 3s: 9 | | | 18 | | | |

Count by 4s: | 16 | 20 | | 28 | | | 40

Count by 10s: 56 | 66 | | | 96 | | 116 |

Complete with <, >, or =.

14 − 7 ◯ 8

10 ◯ 18 − 9

15 − 8 ◯ 7

8 ◯ 13 − 4

Complete.

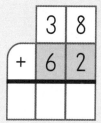

```
    3 8
+   6 2
```

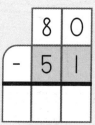

```
    8 0
−   5 1
```

Solve. Write a multiplication problem to match.

RJ filled 4 vases with flowers.
He put 5 flowers in each vase.
How many flowers
did he use?

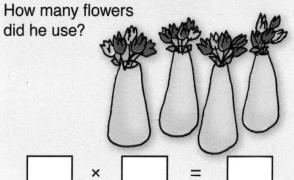

□ × □ = □

Mia's family bought
6 ice cream cones.
Each cone cost $2.
How much did they pay?

$2

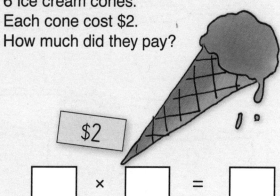

□ × □ = □

Lesson Activities 👥

A

Use Related Addition Facts	Complete a 10

49 + 3 = ☐   49 + 3 = ☐

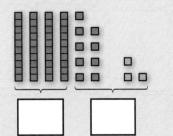

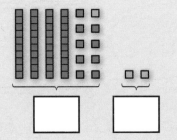

68 + 5 = ☐   77 + 4 = ☐   97 + 6 = ☐

B

Climb and Slide

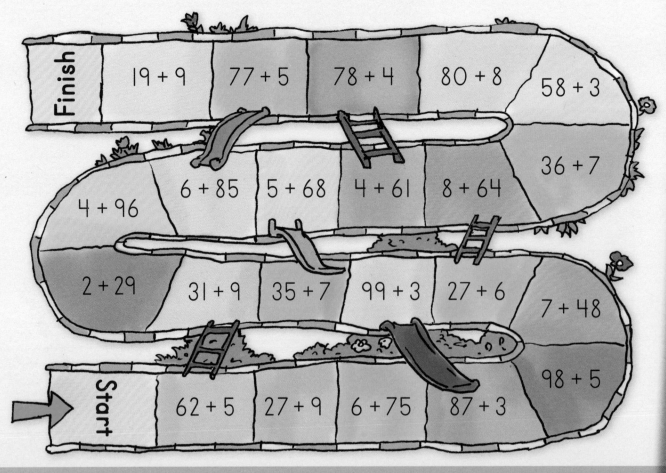

Practice  Complete.

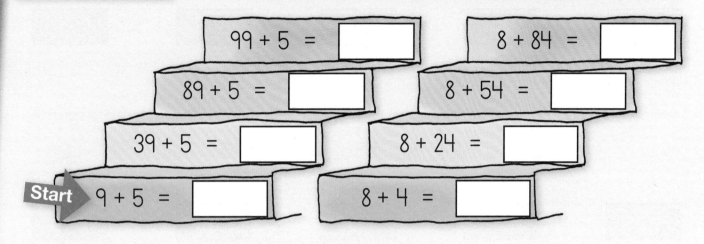

99 + 5 =

89 + 5 =

39 + 5 =

Start 9 + 5 =

8 + 84 =

8 + 54 =

8 + 24 =

8 + 4 =

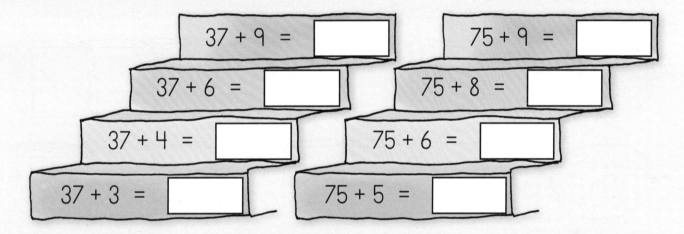

37 + 9 =

37 + 6 =

37 + 4 =

37 + 3 =

75 + 9 =

75 + 8 =

75 + 6 =

75 + 5 =

Solve. Write the equations you use.

Amara has 29 yellow stickers.
She has 8 green stickers.
How many stickers does she have in all?

Rylan has 18 blue robots.
He has 4 more green robots than blue robots.
How many green robots does he have?

 **Review** Connect each number to its dot on the number line.

| 733 | 712 | 763 | 795 | 790 |

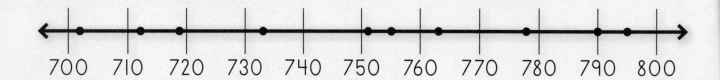

700 710 720 730 740 750 760 770 780 790 800

| 719 | 702 | 751 | 755 | 778 |

Complete the sequences.

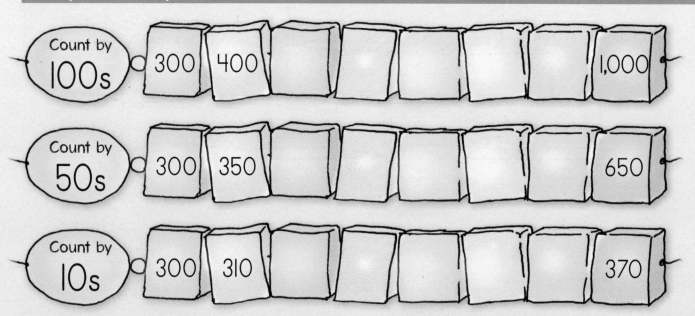

Count by **100s** 300 | 400 | | | | | | 1,000

Count by **50s** 300 | 350 | | | | | | 650

Count by **10s** 300 | 310 | | | | | | 370

Round each number to the nearest ten. | **Complete.**

48	
96	
15	
9	
81	

5 × 4 = ☐   9 × 10 = ☐

2 × 3 = ☐   6 × 5 = ☐

5 × 8 = ☐   3 × 5 = ☐

5 × 9 = ☐   4 × 2 = ☐

8 × 2 = ☐   9 × 0 = ☐

Lesson Activities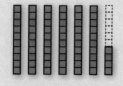

$70 - 6 =$ ☐

$80 - 5 =$ ☐ $30 - 2 =$ ☐ $100 - 7 =$ ☐

B

$72 - 6 =$ ☐

$91 - 5 =$ ☐ $47 - 6 =$ ☐ $83 - 8 =$ ☐

C

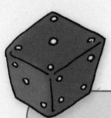

Roll and Subtract

Player 1			Player 2		
82 – ☐	=	☐	82 – ☐	=	☐
60 – ☐	=	☐	60 – ☐	=	☐
41 – ☐	=	☐	41 – ☐	=	☐
57 – ☐	=	☐	57 – ☐	=	☐
100 – ☐	=	☐	100 – ☐	=	☐

Practice 👤 Complete.

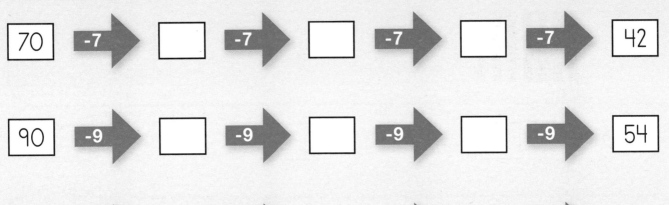

| 70 | -7 → | | -7 → | | -7 → | | -7 → | 42 |

| 90 | -9 → | | -9 → | | -9 → | | -9 → | 54 |

| 80 | -8 → | | -8 → | | -8 → | | -8 → | 48 |

Use the clues to complete the chart.

- Piper is 4 inches shorter than Brayden.

- Leo is 7 inches taller than Piper.

- Josiah is 8 inches taller than Leo.

- Valentina is 6 inches shorter than Josiah.

- Olive is 5 inches shorter than Valentina.

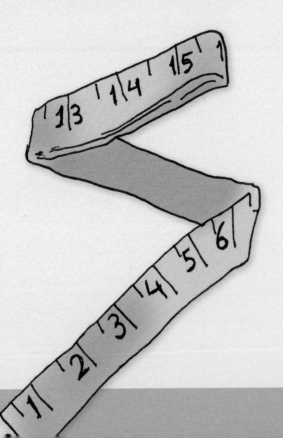

Name	Height (Inches)
Brayden	50
Piper	
Leo	
Josiah	
Valentina	
Olive	

Review 👤 Complete.

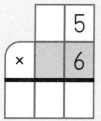 5 × 6 ___

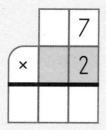 7 × 2 ___

10 × 6 ___

5 × 8 ___

3 × 5 ___

Solve.

You pay the clerk $60.
How much change do you get?

$47

Change
$ ___

You pay the clerk $40.
How much change do you get?

$34

Change
$ ___

Write the time.

 [:] 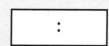 [:]

Complete.

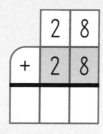

2 8 + 2 8 ___

9 5 − 3 7 ___

Write a multiplication equation to match each array.

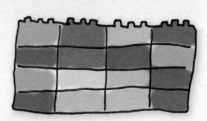

☐ × ☐ = ☐   ☐ × ☐ = ☐   ☐ × ☐ = ☐

Lesson Activities 👥

A

- The chess set costs $20.

- The chess set costs $5 more than the basketball.

- The harmonica costs $10 less than the basketball.

- The harmonica costs $3 more than the markers.

Toy	Price
Chess set	
Basketball	
Harmonica	
Markers	

B

Brielle scored 10 points in a game.
She scored 5 fewer points than her sister.
How many points did her sister score?

Last week, Tomo checked
out 12 library books.
This week, he checked out 5 fewer books
than last week.
How many books did he check out this week?

C

Kendal is 6 years old.
Preston is 7 years older than Kendal.
Grace is 10 years younger than Preston.
How old is Grace?

On Monday, Jake scored 9 points at his
basketball game.
On Tuesday, he scored 4 fewer points
than Monday.
How many points did he score in both
games?

Practice 👤 Use the clues to complete the chart.

- Ben is 3 years older than Leena.

- Leena is 5 years younger than Seth.

- Seth is 8 years younger than Mira.

Name	Age
Ben	8
Leena	
Seth	
Mira	

Solve. Write the equations you use.

Eduardo is 10 years old.
Maria is 3 years younger than Eduardo.
Celeste is 1 year older than Maria.
How old is Celeste?

Nico collected 6 hats for the hat drive.
Cody collected 3 more hats than Nico.
How many did they collect in all?

Complete.

6 → +6 → ☐ → +6 → ☐ → +6 → ☐ → +6 → 30

60 → -6 → ☐ → -6 → ☐ → -6 → ☐ → -6 → 36

Review 👤 Complete the sequences.

Count by 1s: ___ ___ ___ ___ ___ 598 599 600

Count by 2s: ___ ___ ___ ___ ___ 596 598 600

Count by 10s: ___ ___ ___ ___ ___ 580 590 600

Color the problems that match the number in the star.

 **20**

| 5 × 4 |
| 10 × 2 |
| 7 × 2 |

 30

| 10 × 3 |
| 2 × 8 |
| 6 × 5 |

 40

| 8 × 5 |
| 1 × 40 |
| 4 × 10 |

 50

| 10 × 5 |
| 9 × 5 |
| 50 × 1 |

Solve.

Ramona bought 5 books.
Each book cost $5.
How much did she pay?

$5

☐ × ☐ = ☐

Complete.

	Double
8	16
5	
10	
20	
50	
100	
⭐ 150	

Lesson Activities

Split Both Addends

48 + 23 = ☐

40 8 20 3

40 + 20 = ☐
8 + 3 = ☐

Split the Second Addend

48 + 23 = ☐

20 3

48 +20 → ☐ +3 → ☐

35 + 57 = ☐

89 + 15 = ☐

4 | 7 + 6 | 1 = ☐

How close to 100? ☐

1 | 4 + 7 | 6 = ☐

How close to 100? ☐

Close to 100

Sum	Score (How close to 100?)
Player 1 Total	

Sum	Score (How close to 100?)
Player 2 Total	

Practice Match.

64 + 26	90	65 + 34
17 + 82	92	46 + 46
34 + 58	99	38 + 62
57 + 43	100	25 + 77
49 + 53	102	35 + 55

Review 👤 Complete.

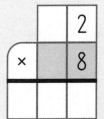 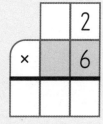

		2
×		8

		4
×		5

	1	0
×		9

		7
×		5

		2
×		6

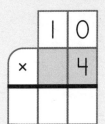 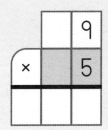 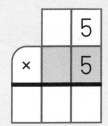 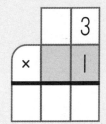

	1	0
×		4

		9
×		5

		5
×		5

		3
×		1

		9
×		2

Use the pictograph to complete the chart.

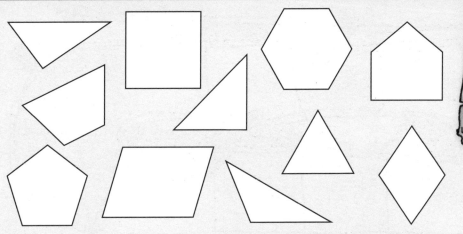

Favorite Color of Apple

Color	Number of People
Red	6
Yellow	
Green	

🍎 = 2 people

Use the key to color the shapes.

Key

Triangle - Red
Quadrilateral - Orange
Pentagon - Green
Hexagon - Blue

Lesson Activities 👥

A

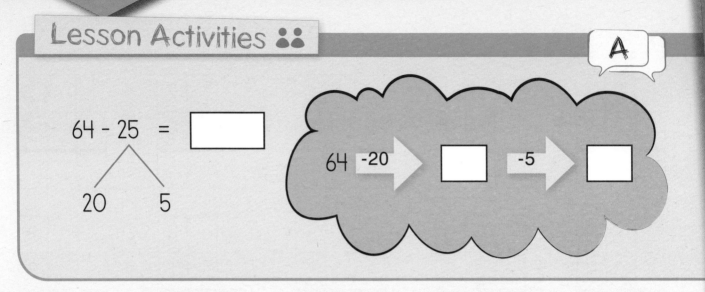

64 – 25 = ☐

20   5

64 **-20** → ☐ **-5** → ☐

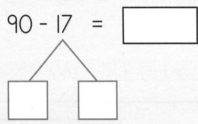

90 – 17 = ☐

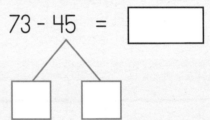

73 – 45 = ☐

B

Climb and Slide

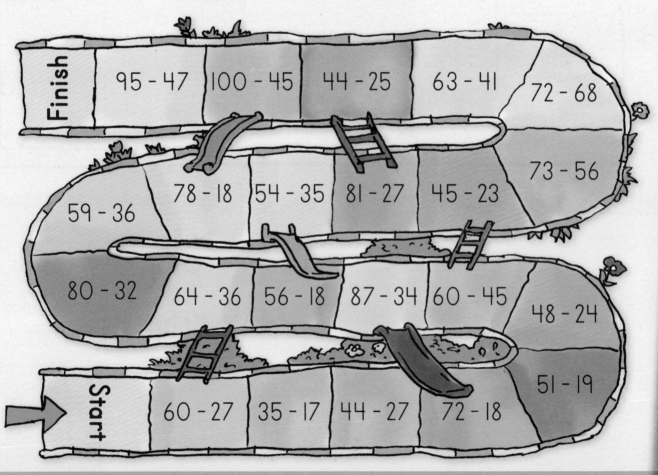

Finish | 95 – 47 | 100 – 45 | 44 – 25 | 63 – 41 | 72 – 68

73 – 56

78 – 18 | 54 – 35 | 81 – 27 | 45 – 23

59 – 36

80 – 32 | 64 – 36 | 56 – 18 | 87 – 34 | 60 – 45

48 – 24

51 – 19

Start | 60 – 27 | 35 – 17 | 44 – 27 | 72 – 18

Practice 👤 Complete.

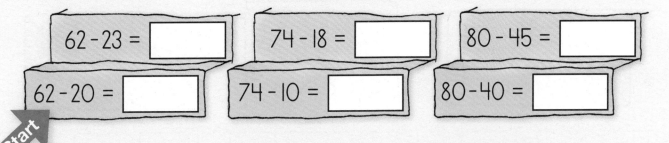

62 − 23 = ☐

62 − 20 = ☐ **Start**

74 − 18 = ☐

74 − 10 = ☐

80 − 45 = ☐

80 − 40 = ☐

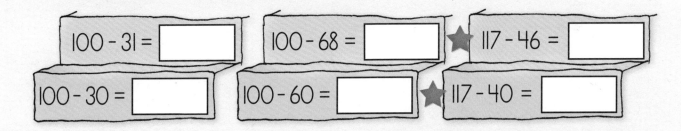

75 − 25 = ☐

75 − 20 = ☐

32 − 16 = ☐

32 − 10 = ☐

53 − 27 = ☐

53 − 20 = ☐

100 − 31 = ☐

100 − 30 = ☐

100 − 68 = ☐

100 − 60 = ☐

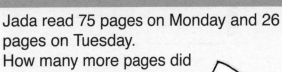 ⭐ 117 − 46 = ☐

⭐ 117 − 40 = ☐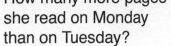

Solve. Write the equations you use.

Jada read 75 pages on Monday and 26 pages on Tuesday. How many pages did she read in all?

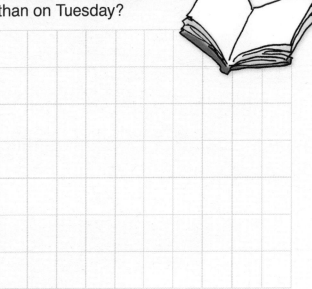

Jada read 75 pages on Monday and 26 pages on Tuesday. How many more pages did she read on Monday than on Tuesday?

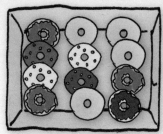

3.7

Review 👤 Write a multiplication equation to match each array.

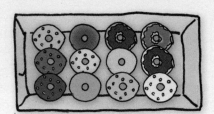 

◻ × ◻ = ◻   ◻ × ◻ = ◻   ◻ × ◻ = ◻

Write each amount of money two ways.   Write a.m. or p.m.

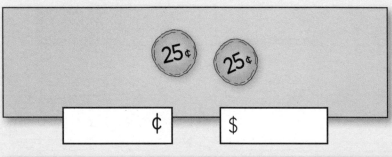

◻ ¢ $ ◻

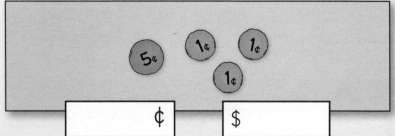

◻ ¢ $ ◻

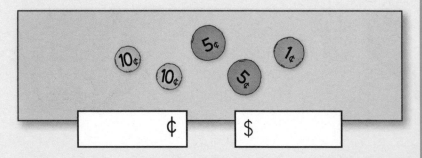

◻ ¢ $ ◻

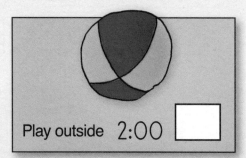

Play outside   2:00 ◻

Bedtime   8:00 ◻

Sunrise   7:00 ◻

Complete.

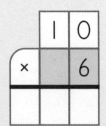

	1	0
×		6

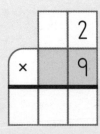

		2
×		9

		7
×		5

		8
×		2

		5
×		9

Lesson Activities

A

52 - 49 = ☐

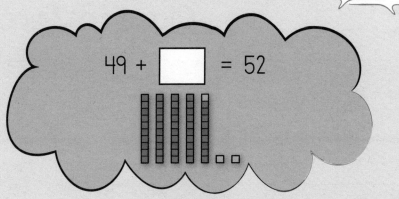

49 + ☐ = 52

---

82 - 75 = ☐

75 + ☐ = 82

64 - 49 = ☐

49 + ☐ = 64

⭐ 104 - 88 = ☐

88 + ☐ = 104

B

| 8 | 9 | - | 6 | 3 | = | ☐ |

| ☐ | ☐ | - | ☐ | ☐ | = | ☐ |

Close to Zero

Difference	Score (How close to zero?)
Player 1 Total	

Difference	Score (How close to zero?)
Player 2 Total	

Practice   Match.

72 – 67	3	84 – 79
43 – 39	4	54 – 50
60 – 45	5	87 – 84
91 – 88	14	72 – 57
51 – 37	15	61 – 47

Review

Complete.

⭐ 11 × 5 = ☐   1 × 5 = ☐

10 × 5 = ☐   2 × 5 = ☐

9 × 5 = ☐   3 × 5 = ☐

8 × 5 = ☐   4 × 5 = ☐

7 × 5 = ☐   5 × 5 = ☐

6 × 5 = ☐

Use the chart to complete the bar graph and answer the questions.

Favorite Ice Cream Flavor

Flavor	Number of People
Strawberry	28
Mint Chip	15
Cookies and Cream	34

Number of People: 40, 30, 20, 10

Flavor: Strawberry, Mint Chip, Cookies and Cream

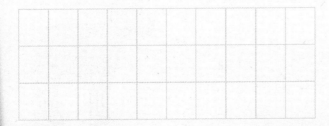

How many more people chose strawberry than mint chip?

How many fewer people chose strawberry than cookies and cream?

Lesson Activities 👥

Taylor read 9 pages on Tuesday morning and 6 pages on Tuesday afternoon.
She read 12 pages on Wednesday.
How many more pages did she read on Tuesday than Wednesday?

Jonah has $7.
He wants to buy a book that costs $6 and an action figure that costs $5.
How much more money does he need?

B

Sadie made 15 cupcakes for the party.
8 had rainbow sprinkles and the rest had chocolate sprinkles.
She ate 2 of the cupcakes with chocolate sprinkles.
How many cupcakes with chocolate sprinkles were left?

There are 14 dogs at the dog park.
9 are big, and the rest are small.
2 more small dogs arrive.
How many small dogs are there now?

Practice 👤 Solve. Write the equations you use.

Kenyana wants to collect 16 hats for the hat drive.
She collected 9 hats on Saturday and 3 hats on Sunday.
How many more hats does she need to collect to meet her goal?

Cayden planted 14 plants.
3 plants were zucchini, and the rest were tomato plants.
Then, 2 tomato plants died.
How many tomato plants were left?

August made 9 clay sculptures.
4 of the sculptures were animals, and the rest were people.
Then, he made 3 more sculptures of people.
How many sculptures of people did he make in all?

Riana painted 13 pictures this week.
She painted 4 pictures on Tuesday and 6 pictures on Friday.
She painted the rest of the pictures on Saturday.
How many pictures did she paint on Saturday?

Review — Complete the sequences.

Count by [ ]s

| | 8 | 12 | | 20 | 24 | | 32 | |

Count by [ ]s

| | | 9 | 12 | 15 | | 21 | | |

Write the time.

[ ]   [ ]   [ ]   [ ]

Complete.

$ [ ]

$ [ ]

Complete.

$5 \times 8 = $ [ ] $8 \times 10 = $ [ ]

$6 \times 2 = $ [ ] $1 \times 5 = $ [ ]

$10 \times 3 = $ [ ] $6 \times 5 = $ [ ]

$5 \times 5 = $ [ ] $5 \times 9 = $ [ ]

$2 \times 8 = $ [ ] $8 \times 0 = $ [ ]

Unit Wrap-Up 👤

Complete. Then, color each answer in black on the 100 Chart to make a picture.

52 + 25 = ☐   65 − 6 = ☐

6 + 57 = ☐   50 − 16 = ☐

48 + 26 = ☐   62 − 25 = ☐

59 + 9 = ☐   93 − 17 = ☐

28 + 47 = ☐   61 − 9 = ☐

1	2	3	4	5	6	7	8	9	10
11	12	13	14	15	16	17	18	19	20
21	22	23	24	25	26	27	28	29	30
31	32	33	34	35	36	37	38	39	40
41	42	43	44	45	46	47	48	49	50
51	52	53	54	55	56	57	58	59	60
61	62	63	64	65	66	67	68	69	70
71	72	73	74	75	76	77	78	79	80
81	82	83	84	85	86	87	88	89	90
91	92	93	94	95	96	97	98	99	100

Unit Wrap-Up 👤 | Complete. | Solve.

10 tens = [ ]

15 tens = [ ]

11 tens = [ ]

18 tens = [ ]

You pay the clerk $100.
How much change do you get?

$82

Change
$ [ ]

Solve. Write the equations you use.

At the movie theater, popcorn costs $6.
Candy costs $3 less than popcorn.
Nachos cost $5 more than candy.
How much do nachos cost?

Mark wants to buy popcorn for $6
and a drink for $5. He has $8.
How much more money does he need?

Hannah collected 24 shells.
She collected 9 on Friday, 7 on Saturday,
and the rest on Sunday.
How many did she collect on Sunday?

Hannah collected 24 shells on the beach.
She collected 7 more shells than her sister.
How many shells did they collect in all?

Lesson Activities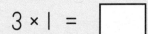

3 × 1 = ☐   3 × 6 = ☐

3 × 2 = ☐   3 × 7 = ☐

3 × 3 = ☐   3 × 8 = ☐

3 × 4 = ☐   3 × 9 = ☐

3 × 5 = ☐   3 × 10 = ☐

2 × 8 = ☐

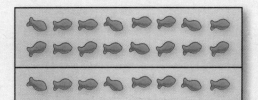

3 × 8 = ☐

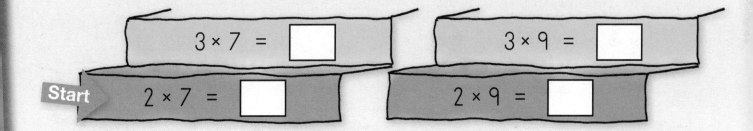

3 × 7 = ☐   3 × 9 = ☐

Start   2 × 7 = ☐   2 × 9 = ☐

Multiplication Cover Up

Player 1

3	6	9	12	15	18	21	24	27	30

Player 2

3	6	9	12	15	18	21	24	27	30

Practice 👤 Complete.

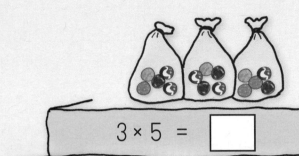

3 × 5 = ☐

2 × 5 = ☐

3 × 4 = ☐

2 × 4 = ☐

3 × 6 = ☐

2 × 6 = ☐

3 × 3 = ☐

2 × 3 = ☐

3 × 8 = ☐

2 × 8 = ☐

3 × 7 = ☐

2 × 7 = ☐

3 × 10 = ☐

2 × 10 = ☐

3 × 9 = ☐

2 × 9 = ☐

Review

Art Supply	Number
Markers	26
Colored Pencils	35
Paint Brushes	8

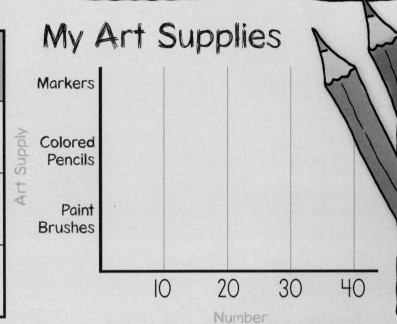

How many markers and colored pencils are there?

How many more colored pencils than markers are there?

Complete.

$34 + \boxed{} = 40$

$34 + \boxed{} = 50$

$34 + \boxed{} = 70$

$34 + \boxed{} = 90$

$34 + \boxed{} = 100$

Write the time.

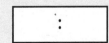 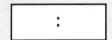

Lesson Activities 👥

$$3 \times 5 = 15$$

Multiples of 5 ➤ | 5 | 10 | 15 | 20 | 25 | 30 | 35 | 40 | 45 | 50 |

Multiples of 2 ➤ | 2 | 4 | 6 | | | | | | | |

Multiples of [ ] ➤ | 3 | 6 | 9 | 12 | 15 | | 21 | | 27 | 30 |

Multiples of [ ] ➤ | 4 | 8 | 12 | 16 | 20 | | | 32 | | |

Tic-Tac-Toe Crash (×3)

18	6	24
27	15	3
21	9	12

Practice 👤 Complete.

Row 1:

× 3 × 3 | × 3 × 8 | × 3 × 2 | × 3 × 9 | × 3 × 4

Row 2:

× 3 × 7 | × 3 × 1 | × 3 × 6 | × 3 × 5 | × 1 0 × 3

Color the multiples in order from Start to End.

Multiples of 2

Start →

2	4	6	11	19
3	25	8	13	37
46	9	10	12	17
1	15	7	14	20 **END**
5	28	41	16	18

Multiples of 5

Start →

10	15	24	49	88
5	20	25	36	16
14	22	30	35	37
72	18	28	40	45
54	32	21	42	50 **END**

Multiples of 3

49	32	28	24	27
50	5	35	21	30 **END**
8	14	20	18	35
6	9	12	15	13
3	11	10	16	8

Start →

Multiples of 4

21	18	44	36	40 **END**
17	35	37	32	45
6	50	25	28	30
4	8	14	24	27
9	12	16	20	25

Start → (points to 4)

Review
Use a ruler to draw a line that matches each length.

5 centimeters

5 inches

Complete the sequences.

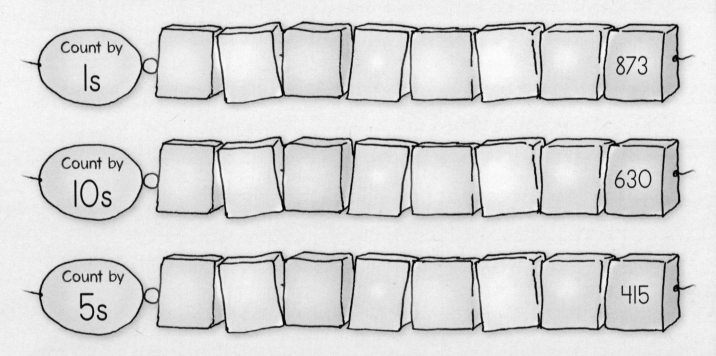

Count by 1s _____ _____ _____ _____ _____ _____ _____ 873

Count by 10s _____ _____ _____ _____ _____ _____ _____ 630

Count by 5s _____ _____ _____ _____ _____ _____ _____ 415

Complete.

	Double
9	
12	
20	
24	
27	

Complete.

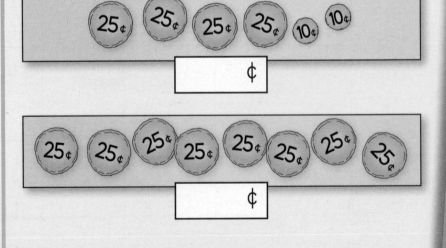

25¢ 25¢ 25¢ 25¢ 10¢ 10¢

_____ ¢

25¢ 25¢ 25¢ 25¢ 25¢ 25¢ 25¢ 25¢

_____ ¢

Lesson Activities 👥

A

$20

2 × 20 = ☐

$50

2 × 50 = ☐

$40

2 × 40 = ☐

B

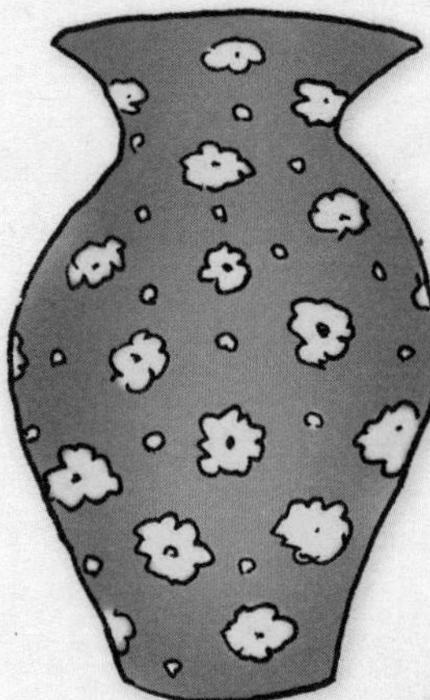

2 × 26 = ☐

20   6

2 × 20 = ☐

2 × 6 = ☐

$14

$28

$37

$59

2 × 14 = ☐

2 × 28 = ☐

2 × 37 = ☐

⭐ 2 × 59 = ☐

Practice 👤 Complete.

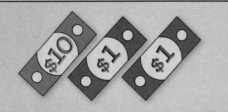

2 × 12 = ☐

2 × 16 = ☐

2 × 24 = ☐

2 × 29 = ☐

2 × 33 = ☐

2 × 45 = ☐

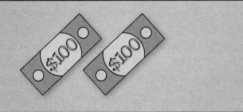

⭐ 2 × 200 = ☐

⭐ 2 × 103 = ☐

Review

Use the pictograph to complete the chart.

Books I've Read

Mystery

Type of Book	Number
Mystery	
Fantasy	
Science	

= 2 books

Write the time.

:

:

:

:

Solve.

You pay the clerk $60.
How much change do you get?

$45

Change
$

Complete the sequences.

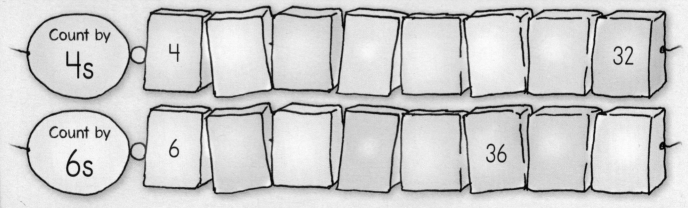

Count by **4s** : 4, , , , , , , 32

Count by **6s** : 6, , , , 36, , ,

Lesson Activities

$4 × 1 = \boxed{}$ $4 × 6 = \boxed{}$

$4 × 2 = \boxed{}$ $4 × 7 = \boxed{}$

$4 × 3 = \boxed{}$ $4 × 8 = \boxed{}$

$4 × 4 = \boxed{}$ $4 × 9 = \boxed{}$

$4 × 5 = \boxed{}$ $4 × 10 = \boxed{}$

B

$2 × 7 = \boxed{}$

$4 × 7 = \boxed{}$

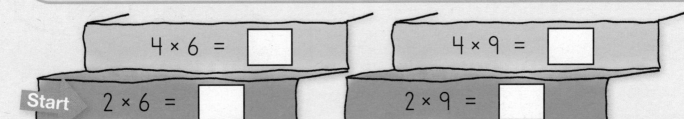

$4 × 6 = \boxed{}$ $4 × 9 = \boxed{}$

Start $2 × 6 = \boxed{}$ $2 × 9 = \boxed{}$

C

Multiplication Crash

4	8	12	16	20
24	28	32	36	40

Practice   Complete.

4 × 2 = ☐

4 × 3 = ☐

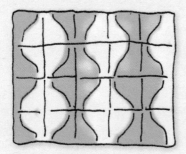

4 × 5 = ☐

4 × 8 = ☐

4 × 9 = ☐

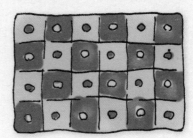

4 × 6 = ☐

4 × 4 = ☐

4 × 7 = ☐

4.4

Review

Complete.

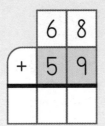

```
    6 8
  + 5 9
  -------
```

```
    7 4
  - 2 8
  -------
```

Copy the shapes.

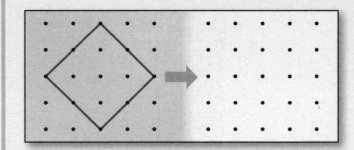

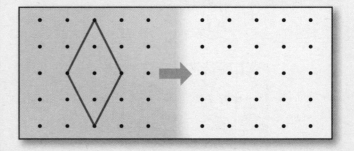

Complete.

1 minute = ☐ seconds

1 hour = ☐ minutes

1 day = ☐ hours

1 week = ☐ days

Complete.

$ ☐

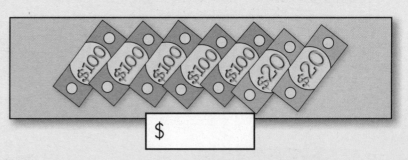

$ ☐

Circle the sandwiches that are split in half. X the sandwiches that are not split in half.

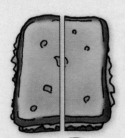    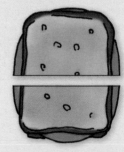

Lesson Activities 👥

Multiplication Undercover

Player 1	4	8	12	16	20	24	28	32	36	40
Player 2	4	8	12	16	20	24	28	32	36	40

Donut Sales

Friday | ⊙ ⊙ ⊙
Saturday | ⊙ ⊙ ⊙ ⊙ ⊙ ⊙
Sunday | ⊙ ⊙ ⊙ ⊙ ⊙

⊙ = 10 donuts

Day	Multiplication Problem	Number of Donuts
Friday		
Saturday		
Sunday		

Pony Rides

Friday | 🎟 🎟 🎟 🎟 🎟
Saturday | 🎟 🎟 🎟 🎟
Sunday | 🎟 🎟

🎟 = 5 tickets

Day	Multiplication Problem	Number of Tickets
Friday		
Saturday		
Sunday		

Practice

Use the pictograph to answer the questions.
Write a multiplication equation for each question.

Pumpkins Sold

Friday

Saturday

Sunday

= 3 pumpkins

How many pumpkins were sold on Friday?

☐ × ☐ = ☐

How many pumpkins were sold on Saturday?

☐ × ☐ = ☐

How many pumpkins were sold on Sunday?

☐ × ☐ = ☐

Complete.

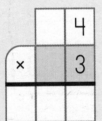
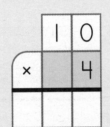
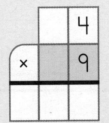
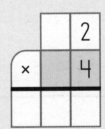
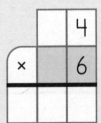

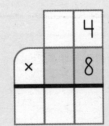
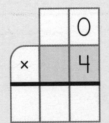
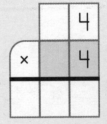

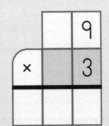

Lesson 4.5

Review 👤 Complete.

	2	9
+	4	8

	6	5
+	3	5

	4	2
−	1	6

	8	0
−	2	7

Write the time.

[:]

[:]

[:]

[:]

Complete.

17 tens = [ ]

14 tens = [ ]

[ ] tens = 150

[ ] tens = 190

⭐ [ ] tens = 560

⭐ 38 tens = [ ]

Solve. Write the equations you use.

The sum of 2 numbers is 20.
One of the numbers is 11.
What is the other number?

⭐ The sum of 3 numbers is 24.
One of the numbers is 8.
Another one of the numbers is 7.
What is the other number?

4.6

Lesson Activities 👥

Dice Tic-Tac-Toe

8 × 2	9 × 5	4 × 4	6 × 0	6 × 4
5 × 3	8 × 4	7 × 2	7 × 3	8 × 5
9 × 4	5 × 5	8 × 3	6 × 5	7 × 4
7 × 5	9 × 3	7 × 10	5 × 4	6 × 5
8 × 1	3 × 4	3 × 3	9 × 2	6 × 3

B

×	1	2	3	4	5	6	7	8	9	10
1	1	2	3	4	5	6	7		9	10
2	2	4	6	8	10		14	16	18	20
3	3		9	12	15	18	21	24		30
4	4	8	12	16		24	28	32	36	40
5	5	10	15	20	25	30	35	40	45	50
6	6	12	18	24	30	36	42	48	54	60
7	7	14	21	28		42	49	56	63	70
8	8		24	32	40	48	56	64	72	
9	9	18	27		45	54	63	72	81	90
10	10	20	30	40	50	60	70		90	100

Practice 👤 Complete.

3 × 5 = ☐   4 × 5 = ☐   3 × 6 = ☐

4 × 3 = ☐   3 × 7 = ☐   4 × 4 = ☐

3 × 9 = ☐   10 × 3 = ☐   3 × 8 = ☐

6 × 4 = ☐   7 × 5 = ☐   4 × 10 = ☐

5 × 9 = ☐   4 × 9 = ☐   5 × 6 = ☐

8 × 4 = ☐   5 × 5 = ☐   7 × 4 = ☐

Solve. Write a multiplication equation to match.

Xavier made 4 treat bags for a party.
Each treat bag had 3 lollipops.
How many lollipops did he use?

Lauren bought 3 pumpkins.
Each pumpkin cost $6.
How much did the pumpkins cost in all?

☐ × ☐ = ☐   ☐ × ☐ = ☐

Review

Use the numbers to complete the blanks.
You will use each number once.

| 10 | 20 | 30 | 40 | 50 | 60 | 70 | 80 | 90 |

30 + ☐ = 50   ☐ - 40 = 20   100 = ☐ + 60

90 - ☐ = 10   ☐ + 50 = 60   40 = ☐ - 30

50 + ☐ = 80   ☐ - 20 = 70   60 = ☐ + 10

Complete.

1 foot = ☐ inches

1 yard = ☐ feet

1 yard = ☐ inches

1 meter = ☐ centimeters

Solve. Write the equation you use.

Ben had $90. Then, he spent $67.
How much money did he have left?

Complete.

47 - 9 = ☐   53 - 26 = ☐   60 - 24 = ☐

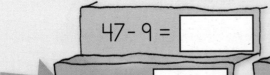

Start 47 - 7 = ☐   53 - 20 = ☐   60 - 4 = ☐

Unit Wrap-Up — Complete.

		4
×	1	0

	3
×	5

	4
×	7

	6
×	3

	3
×	4

	7
×	3

	9
×	4

	3
×	8

	4
×	5

	1	0
×		3

	4
×	4

	3
×	9

	4
×	8

	4
×	3

	4
×	6

Complete the multiples in order.

Multiples of 2 → | 2 | 4 | | | 10 | | | 16 | | |

Multiples of 5 → | | 10 | 15 | | | 30 | | | | |

Use the words in the word bank to complete the sentences.

$$2 \times 7 = 14$$

Word bank:
- factors
- product

14 is the _____.

2 and 7 are the _____.

Unit Wrap-Up

Use the pictograph to answer the questions. Write a multiplication equation to match each question.

Isabella's Piano Practice

Monday	♪ ♪ ♪ ♪ ♪ ♪
Tuesday	♪ ♪ ♪
Wednesday	♪ ♪ ♪ ♪ ♪ ♪ ♪

♪ = 5 minutes

How many minutes did Isabella practice on Monday?

☐ × ☐ = ☐

How many minutes did Isabella practice on Tuesday?

☐ × ☐ = ☐

How many minutes did Isabella practice on Wednesday?

☐ × ☐ = ☐

Complete.

2 × 35 = ☐

2 × 46 = ☐

2 × 31 = ☐

2 × 45 = ☐

Start 2 × 30 = ☐

2 × 40 = ☐

Solve. Write the equations you use.

Ellie has 6 bags of candy.
Each bag has 4 pieces of candy.
How many pieces of candy does she have?

Joey wants to make 3 spider crafts.
Each spider uses 8 craft sticks.
How many craft sticks does Joey need?

Lesson Activities 👥

A

Number Riddles

217   450

699   864   8   603   271

99   701   630   1,000   375

B

324 = [   ]   506 = [   ]

C

⟵|————————————————|⟶
600   700

628 Cotton Balls

About [   ] cotton balls

$693

About [   ] dollars

655 KILOMETERS

About [   ] kilometers

D

⟵|——|——|——|——|——|——|——|——|——|——|⟶
0   100 200 300 400 500 600 700 800 900 1,000

482	249	301	532	299	850	940	984

Practice 👤 Connect each number to its dot on the number line.

248   260   325   372   398

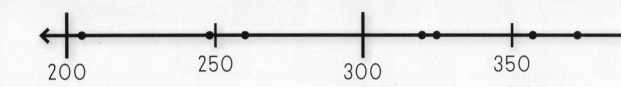

205   320   357

Round each number to the nearest hundred. Use the number line to help.

325	248	260	205	372	357	398	320

Round each number to the nearest hundred.

About [   ] blocks

About [   ] stickers

About [   ] rubber bands

About [   ] paper clips

Review 👤 Match pairs that equal 100.

| 50 | 55 | 60 | 65 | 70 |

| 45 | 30 | 50 | 35 | 40 |

Complete.

Expanded Form	Number
300 + 20 + 5	325
600 + 80 + 9	
100 + 40 + 6	
	299
700 + 4	
	980

Complete.

$ [____]

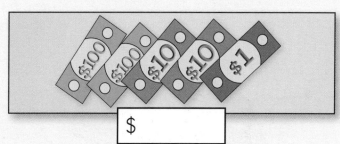

$ [____]

Complete with <, >, or =.

400 + 50 ◯ 449

900 − 600 ◯ 400

560 ◯ 500 + 6

705 ◯ 700 + 5

Complete.

94 + [____] = 100

32 + [____] = 40

71 + [____] = 80

85 + [____] = 100

5.2

You have saved $280.
How much more money do you need?

$$280 + \boxed{} = 300$$

$$80 + \boxed{} = 100$$

$$650 + \boxed{} = 700$$

$$460 + \boxed{} = 500$$

You have saved $680.
How much more money do you need?

$$680 + \boxed{} = 1{,}000$$

$$680 + \boxed{} \; 700 + \boxed{} \; 1{,}000$$

$$450 + \boxed{} = 1{,}000$$

$$450 + \boxed{} \; 500 + \boxed{} \; 1{,}000$$

$$790 + \boxed{} = 1{,}000$$

$$790 + \boxed{} \; 800 + \boxed{} \; 1{,}000$$

Practice

Match pairs that equal 1,000.

900	300
700	50
800	100
950	250
750	200
850	150

Complete.

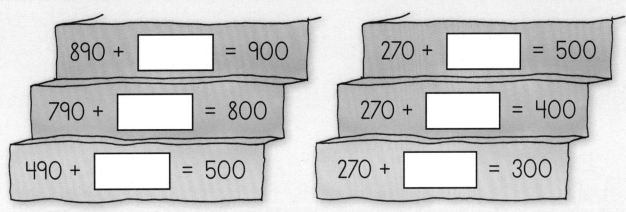

890 + [ ] = 900   270 + [ ] = 500

790 + [ ] = 800   270 + [ ] = 400

490 + [ ] = 500   270 + [ ] = 300

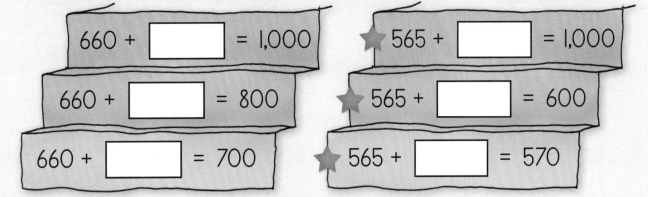

660 + [ ] = 1,000   ★ 565 + [ ] = 1,000

660 + [ ] = 800   ★ 565 + [ ] = 600

660 + [ ] = 700   ★ 565 + [ ] = 570

Review

Color the problems that match the number in the star.

| 4 × 3 |
| 2 × 9 |
| 2 × 6 |

| 8 × 2 |
| 4 × 4 |
| 6 × 0 |

| 2 × 9 |
| 5 × 4 |
| 3 × 6 |

| 4 × 5 |
| 7 × 1 |
| 10 × 2 |

| 6 × 4 |
| 2 × 12 |
| 8 × 3 |

| 2 × 14 |
| 7 × 4 |
| 5 × 5 |

| 3 × 9 |
| 4 × 8 |
| 2 × 16 |

| 2 × 20 |
| 8 × 5 |
| 3 × 10 |

Solve. Write a multiplication equation to match.

Chloe arranged her stickers in 4 rows and 5 columns. How many stickers did she use?

Diego planted 3 rows of flowers. Each row had 6 flowers. How many flowers did he plant?

☐ × ☐ = ☐

☐ × ☐ = ☐

Lesson Activities 👥

Multiplication Crash

4	8	12	16	20
24	28	32	36	40

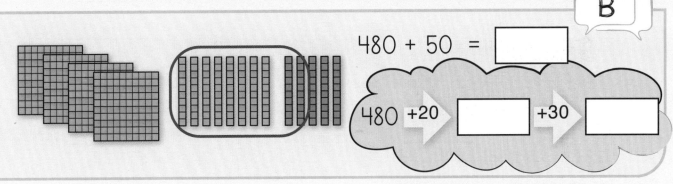

480 + 50 = ☐

480 → +20 → ☐ → +30 → ☐

290 + 30 = ☐   760 + 70 = ☐

180 + 80 = ☐   370 + 40 = ☐

330 − 50 = ☐

330 → −30 → ☐ → −20 → ☐

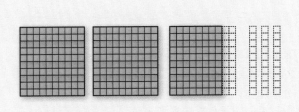

210 − 40 = ☐   550 − 60 = ☐

430 − 50 = ☐   820 − 90 = ☐

Practice 👤 Complete.

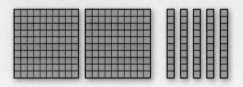

250 + 30 = ☐

250 + 50 = ☐

250 + 60 = ☐

250 + 90 = ☐

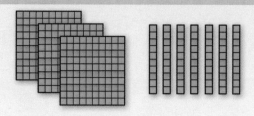

370 + 20 = ☐

370 + 30 = ☐

370 + 50 = ☐

370 + 80 = ☐

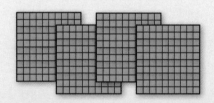

400 - 10 = ☐

400 - 40 = ☐

400 - 70 = ☐

400 - 90 = ☐

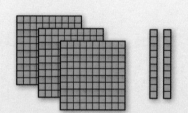

320 - 20 = ☐

320 - 30 = ☐

320 - 40 = ☐

320 - 70 = ☐

Solve. Write the equations you use.

Gabriella read 150 pages on Monday.
She read 80 pages on Tuesday.
How many pages did she read in all?

Gabriella read 150 pages on Monday.
She read 80 pages on Tuesday.
How many more pages did she read on
Monday than on Tuesday?

Review  Write each number in its expanded form.

717 = ⬚

707 = ⬚

770 = ⬚

Complete.

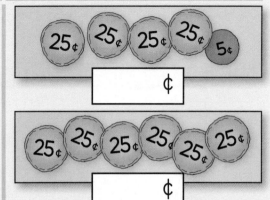

⬚ ¢

⬚ ¢

Connect each number to its dot on the number line.

| 625 | 612 | 658 | 682 | 690 |

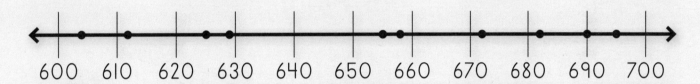

600 610 620 630 640 650 660 670 680 690 700

| 604 | 629 | 655 | 672 | 695 |

Write the time.

⬚ : ⬚

⬚ : ⬚

⬚ : ⬚

⬚ : ⬚

Complete.

	7	4
+	2	9

	8	8
+	8	8

5.4

Lesson Activities

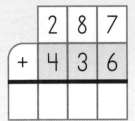

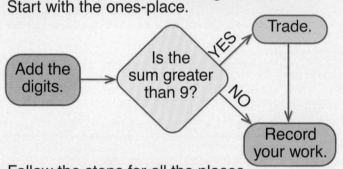

The Addition Algorithm

* * * Start with the ones-place.

Add the digits. → Is the sum greater than 9? — YES → Trade. — Record your work. / NO → Record your work.

* * * Follow the steps for all the places.

Leaf Fight

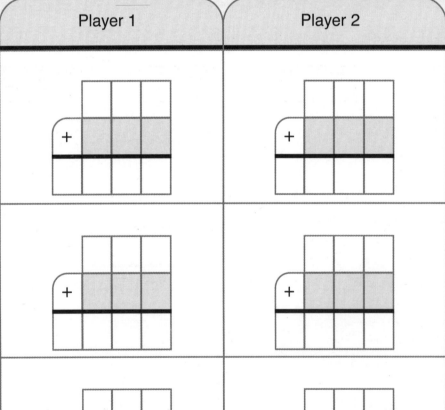

Player 1	Player 2

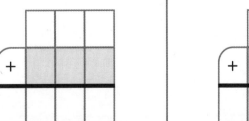

Practice 👤 Complete.

	2	9	5
+	3	4	7

	5	6	1
+	2	3	8

	4	4	6
+	3	5	4

Solve. Write the equations you use.

Zari's family drove 275 miles in the morning and 148 miles in the afternoon. How far did they drive that day?

Charlie's family drove 362 miles to his grandparents' house. Then, they drove 362 miles back to their home. How far did they drive in all?

Review 👤 Write the multiples in order.

Multiples of 3	3	6		12		18		24		

Multiples of 4	4			16	20		28			

Round to the nearest hundred.

401	682	949	951	550	234

Lesson Activities 👥

A

Design Your OWN PLAYSET!

Tire swing $235

Swing $73

Slide $358

Climbing net $226

Spiral slide $467

How much does it cost to buy a tire swing and a spiral slide?

Estimate

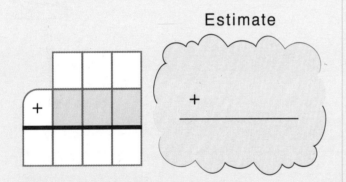

+ _____

How much does it cost to buy a climbing net and a tire swing?

Estimate

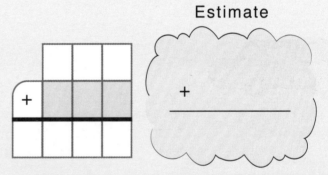

+ _____

How much does it cost to buy a regular slide and a spiral slide?

Estimate

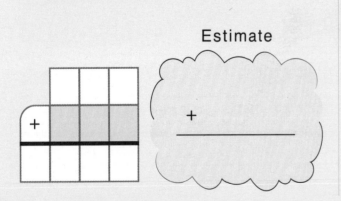

+ _____

Choose 3 items you would like to have in a playset. How much would it cost to buy all 3?

Estimate

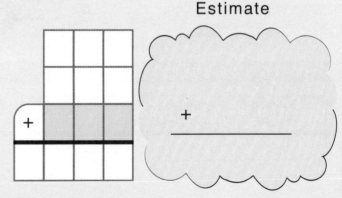

+ _____

Practice 👤 Complete.

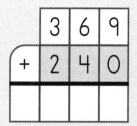

```
  3 6 9
+ 2 4 0
_____
```

```
  6 0 5
+ 3 9 4
_____
```

```
  4 9 5
+ 1 7 5
_____
```

Clara solved these problems, but she made some mistakes. Estimate the sum for each problem and check her work. Mark whether each answer is correct or incorrect.

Estimate

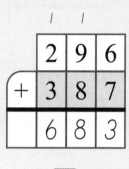

```
   2 9 6
+  3 8 7
_____
   6 8 3
```

+ _____

☐ Correct   ☐ Incorrect

Estimate

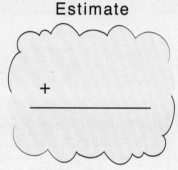

```
   5 1 7
+  2 2 7
_____
   8 4 4
```

+ _____

☐ Correct   ☐ Incorrect

Estimate

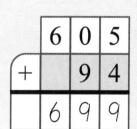

```
   6 0 5
+    9 4
_____
   6 9 9
```

+ _____

☐ Correct   ☐ Incorrect

Estimate

```
   4 6 8
+  3 2 9
_____
   6 9 7
```

+ _____

☐ Correct   ☐ Incorrect

Estimate

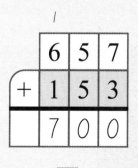

```
   6 5 7
+  1 5 3
_____
   7 0 0
```

+ _____

☐ Correct   ☐ Incorrect

Estimate

```
   8 7 3
+  1 0 2
_____
   6 7 1
```

+ _____

☐ Correct   ☐ Incorrect

Review — Complete.

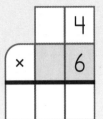

	4
×	6

	3
×	7

	5
×	6

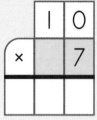

	1 0
×	7

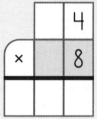

	4
×	8

	4
×	7

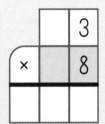

	3
×	8

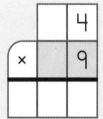

	4
×	9

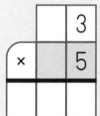

	3
×	5

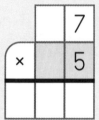

	7
×	5

Maya made a pictograph to show how long she exercised. Use the pictograph to answer the questions. Write a multiplication equation for each question.

My Exercise

Tuesday	■ ■ ■ ■ ■
Wednesday	■ ■ ■ ■ ■ ■ ■
Thursday	■ ■ ■ ■ ■ ■

■ = 5 minutes

How many minutes did Maya exercise on Tuesday?

☐ × ☐ = ☐

How many minutes did Maya exercise on Wednesday?

☐ × ☐ = ☐

How many minutes did Maya exercise on Thursday?

☐ × ☐ = ☐

Complete.

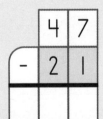

4	7
− 2	1

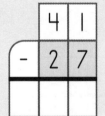

4	1
− 2	7

Solve.

You pay the clerk $80.
How much change do you get?

$67

Change
$ ☐

Lesson Activities

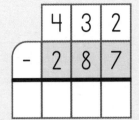

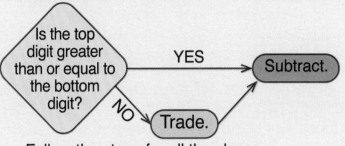

The Subtraction Algorithm

★ ★ ★ Start with the ones-place.

Is the top digit greater than or equal to the bottom digit?

YES → Subtract.

NO → Trade. → Subtract.

★ ★ ★ Follow the steps for all the places.

SPIN TO WIN!

812   784
535   628
943   590

451   276
375   281   142
429

Player 1	Player 2

Practice 🔹 Complete.

	9	4	7
-	6	8	2

	3	5	1
-	1	2	6

	8	3	0
-	4	5	8

Solve. Write the equations you use.

Jaydan's family drove 447 miles on Monday and 375 miles on Tuesday. How much further did they drive on Monday than Tuesday?

Daniela's cousin lives 550 miles away. After her family drives 236 miles, how much further do they need to drive to get to her cousins' house?

Review 🔹 Complete the missing numbers.

×	1	2	3	4	5	6	7	8	9	10
1	1	2	3	4	5	6	7	8	9	10
2	2	4	6	8	10	12		16	18	20
3	3	6	9	12	15		21	24	27	30
4	4	8		16	20	24		32		40
5	5		15	20		30	35	40	45	50
6	6	12	18	24	30	36	42	48	54	
7	7	14		28	35	42	49	56	63	70
8		16	24		40	48	56	64	72	80
9	9	18		36	45	54	63	72	81	90
10	10		30	40	50	60	70	80	90	

Lesson Activities

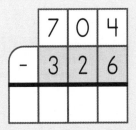

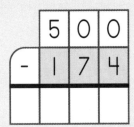

The Subtraction Algorithm

* * * Start with the ones-place.

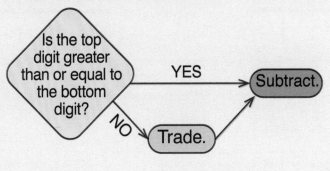

Is the top digit greater than or equal to the bottom digit?

YES → Subtract.

NO → Trade. → Subtract.

* * * Follow the steps for all the places.

Design Your OWN PLAYSET!

Tire swing $235

Swing $73

Climbing net $226

Slide $358

Spiral slide $467

How much more does a spiral slide cost than a climbing net?

Estimate

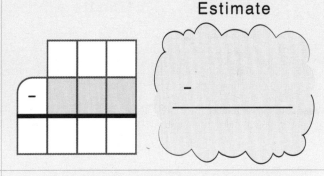

You have $600. Then, you buy a climbing net. How much money do you have left?

Estimate

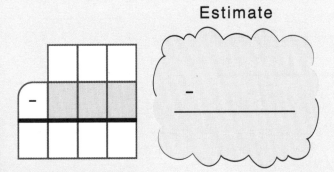

You have $300. Then, you buy a regular swing. How much money do you have left?

Estimate

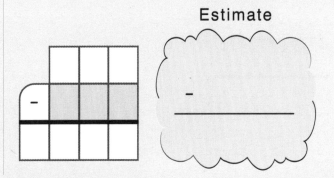

5.7

Practice Complete.

```
  5 6 0
-  3 1 2
─────────

```

```
  4 0 0
-  2 8 3
─────────

```

```
  6 0 3
-  2 4 9
─────────

```

Xander solved these problems, but he made some mistakes. Estimate the difference for each problem and check his work. Mark whether each answer is correct or incorrect.

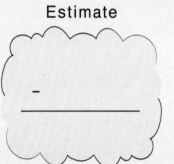

Estimate

_____ - _____

☐ Correct   ☐ Incorrect

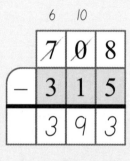

Estimate

_____ - _____

☐ Correct   ☐ Incorrect

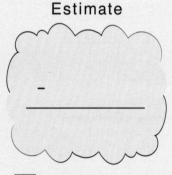

Estimate

_____ - _____

☐ Correct   ☐ Incorrect

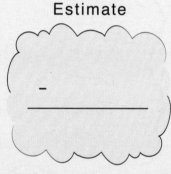

Estimate

_____ - _____

☐ Correct   ☐ Incorrect

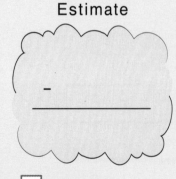

Estimate

_____ - _____

☐ Correct   ☐ Incorrect

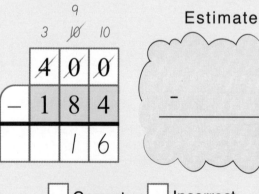

Estimate

_____ - _____

☐ Correct   ☐ Incorrect

Review

Use the key to color the leaves.

Key
Even - Red
Odd - Orange

Leaves: 7, 968, 203, 350, 499, 245, 777, 81, 106

Complete.

9 × 5 = ☐   4 × 7 = ☐

8 × 4 = ☐   3 × 9 = ☐

3 × 7 = ☐   2 × 8 = ☐

6 × 4 = ☐   10 × 7 = ☐

5 × 5 = ☐   4 × 9 = ☐

Write each money amount two ways.

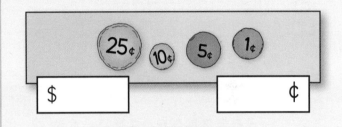

$ ☐   ☐ ¢

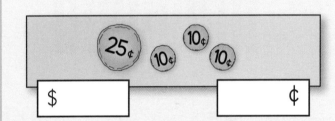

$ ☐   ☐ ¢

Solve.

You want to buy a bike that costs $300.
You have $260.
How much more money do you need?

$300

Complete.

9 tens = ☐

10 tens = ☐

11 tens = ☐

15 tens = ☐

18 tens = ☐

Lesson Activities 👥

A

Roll and Multiply

	Score
6 × ▭	
7 × ▭	
8 × ▭	
9 × ▭	

Player 1 Total

	Score
6 × ▭	
7 × ▭	
8 × ▭	
9 × ▭	

Player 2 Total

B

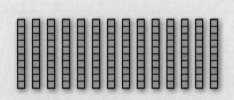

14 × 10 = ▭

14 tens = ▭

23 × 10 = ▭   46 × 10 = ▭   58 × 10 = ▭

C

Shopping List

16 bags of oranges

▭ × ▭ = ▭ oranges

24 boxes of granola bars

▭ × ▭ = ▭ granola bars

30 cases of water

▭ × ▭ = ▭ bottles of water

Practice 👤 Complete.

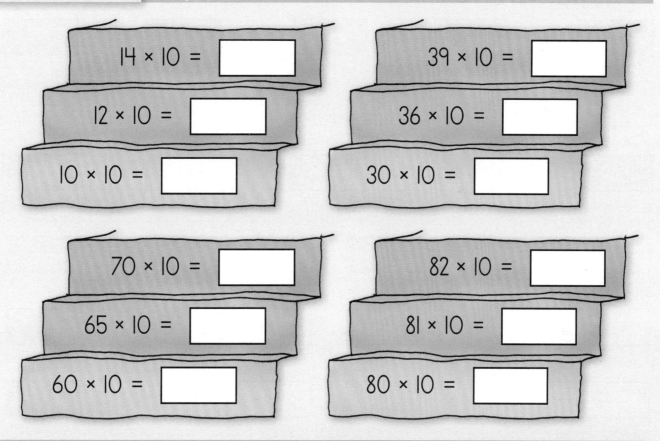

14 × 10 = ☐

12 × 10 = ☐

10 × 10 = ☐

39 × 10 = ☐

36 × 10 = ☐

30 × 10 = ☐

70 × 10 = ☐

65 × 10 = ☐

60 × 10 = ☐

82 × 10 = ☐

81 × 10 = ☐

80 × 10 = ☐

Solve. Write the equations you use.

Movie tickets cost $10.
How much do 34 tickets cost?

The theater has 25 rows.
Each row has 10 chairs.
How many chairs are there?

There are 10 paper plates in each pack.
Zahra buys 18 packs.
How many paper plates does she get?

Benjamin's mom drives 10 miles
for work every day.
How many miles does she drive
in 30 work days?

5.8

| 750 | 770 | 775 | 799 | 790 |

| 50 | 25 | 30 | 10 | 1 |

Match.

5×9		21
4×8		30
7×3		45
5×6		32
3×8		24

7×4		24
9×3		28
4×6		27
3×6		35
5×7		18

Solve. Write the equations you use.

The choir sold 148 adult tickets and 94 child tickets for the concert.
How many more adult tickets than child tickets did they sell?

The choir sold 148 adult tickets and 94 child tickets for the concert.
How many tickets did they sell in all?

Lesson Activities 👥

A

$3 \times 40 = \boxed{}$

$3 \times 4 \text{ tens} = \boxed{} \text{ tens}$

$2 \times 90 = \boxed{}$

$2 \times 9 \text{ tens} = \boxed{} \text{ tens}$

$8 \times 20 = \boxed{}$

$8 \times 2 \text{ tens} = \boxed{} \text{ tens}$

$5 \times 60 = \boxed{}$

$5 \times 6 \text{ tens} = \boxed{} \text{ tens}$

B

Four in a Row

3×70	200	5×50	160	4×80
100	270	160	150	10×20
120	500	320	2×50	50×10
8×20	200	210	200	4×40
6×20	250	4×50	9×30	5×30

Practice 👤 Match.

| 2 × 50 | | 18 × 10 |

160

| 4 × 40 | | 4 × 30 |

180

| 20 × 10 | | 2 × 80 |

100

| 6 × 20 | | 5 × 20 |

200

120

| 2 × 90 | | 5 × 40 |

Solve. Write the equations you use.

Tiana's parents buy 4 concert tickets.
Each ticket costs $70.
How much do the tickets cost in all?

Jackson likes to make crafts with yarn.
He uses 50 inches of yarn for each craft.
How much yarn does he need to make
4 crafts?

The theater has 5 sections.
Each section has 80 seats.
How many seats are in the theater?

 There are 60 minutes in 1 hour.
How many minutes are in 4 hours?

Review

Draw a shape to match.

Triangle

Rectangle

Square

Complete.

	5	6	7
+	3	3	3

	7	0	0
−	4	8	1

Match.

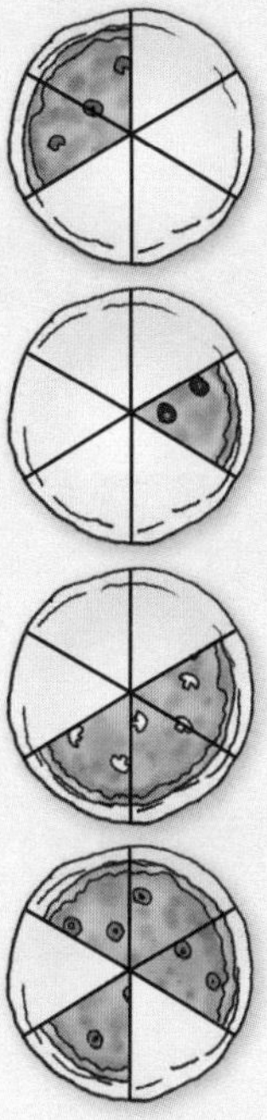

$\frac{1}{6}$

$\frac{2}{6}$

$\frac{3}{6}$

$\frac{4}{6}$

Complete the sequences.

Count by **100s**

317 _ _ _ _ 817

Count by **10s**

317 _ _ _ _ 367

Unit Wrap-Up 👤

Complete.

$380 + \boxed{} = 400$

$590 + \boxed{} = 600$

$750 + \boxed{} = 800$

$750 + \boxed{} = 1{,}000$

Complete.

	+40
600	
460	
590	
750	
880	
370	

Match.

570 + 30		650 - 60
	580	
550 + 40		640 - 30
	590	
580 + 30		620 - 40
	600	
510 + 70		630 - 30
	610	
590 + 30		700 - 80
	620	

Unit Wrap-Up Estimate the answer to each problem. Then, find the exact answer.

Estimate

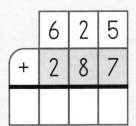

+ _____

Estimate

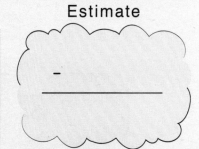

- _____

Estimate

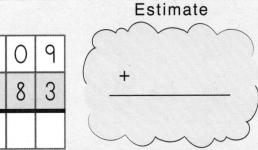

+ _____

Estimate

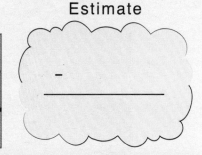

- _____

Color the problems that equal the number in the star.

200

| 4 × 50 |
| 20 × 10 |
| 30 × 6 |

240

| 60 × 4 |
| 40 × 6 |
| 70 × 3 |

280

| 4 × 70 |
| 8 × 40 |
| 28 × 10 |

400

| 40 × 10 |
| 20 × 4 |
| 8 × 50 |

Solve. Write the equations you use.

The ballet school sold 356 tickets to the performance. 149 were child tickets, and the rest were adult tickets.
How many were adult tickets?

Makayla's mom bought 22 tickets to the ballet performance. Each ticket cost $10. How much did she pay for the tickets?

Lesson Activities 👥

Escape the Maze (×3)

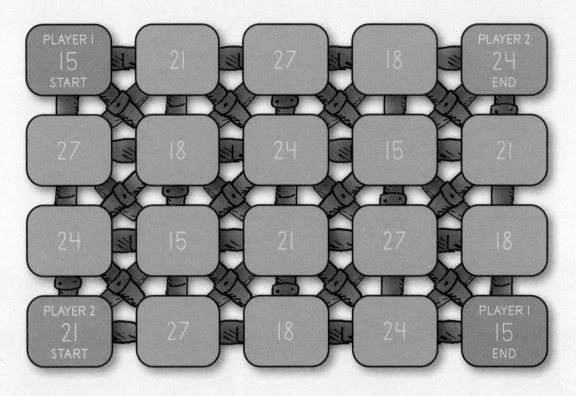

PLAYER 1 15 START	21	27	18	PLAYER 2 24 END
27	18	24	15	21
24	15	21	27	18
PLAYER 2 21 START	27	18	24	PLAYER 1 15 END

Recipe
1½ cups flour
¾ cup sugar

Nature Trail
2½ miles

| Halves | Thirds | Fourths | Sixths |

Practice 👤 Circle the shapes that are split into thirds.
X the shapes that are not split into thirds.

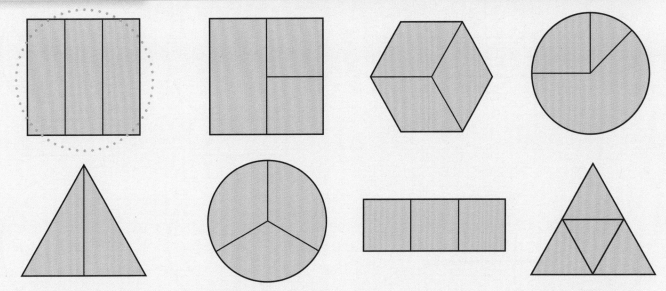

Circle the shapes that are cut into sixths. X the shapes that are not cut into sixths.

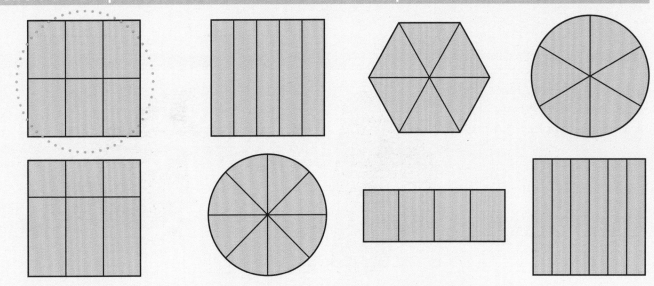

Review   Complete.

560 + 80 = ☐   740 - 80 = ☐

560 + 50 = ☐   740 - 50 = ☐

560 + 40 = ☐   740 - 40 = ☐

Complete.   Write the time.

	3	8	5
+	2	4	5

	6	0	0
-	3	2	6

__ : __   __ : __

__ : __   __ : __

Solve. Write a multiplication equation.

Max bought 3 packs of pencils.
Each pack had 20 pencils.
How many pencils did he buy?

☐ × ☐ = ☐

Viv bought 4 boxes of paper clips.
Each box had 50 paper clips.
How many paper clips did she buy?

☐ × ☐ = ☐

Lesson Activities 👥

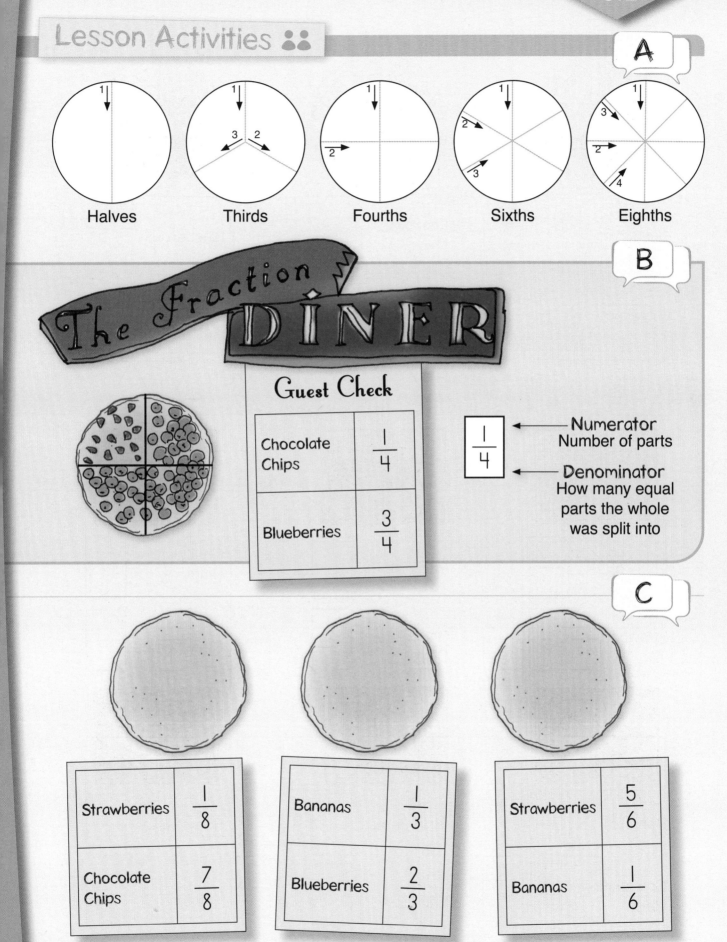

Halves   Thirds   Fourths   Sixths   Eighths

B

The Fraction DINER

Guest Check

| Chocolate Chips | $\frac{1}{4}$ |
| Blueberries | $\frac{3}{4}$ |

$\frac{1}{4}$ ← Numerator
Number of parts

← Denominator
How many equal parts the whole was split into

C

| Strawberries | $\frac{1}{8}$ |
| Chocolate Chips | $\frac{7}{8}$ |

| Bananas | $\frac{1}{3}$ |
| Blueberries | $\frac{2}{3}$ |

| Strawberries | $\frac{5}{6}$ |
| Bananas | $\frac{1}{6}$ |

D

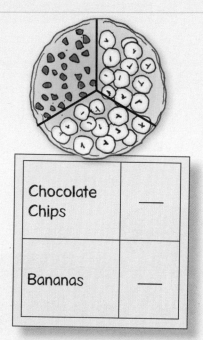

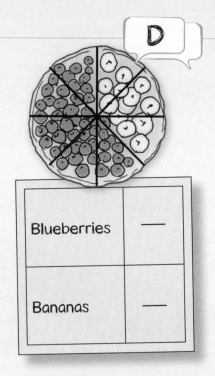

Blueberries	——	Chocolate Chips	——	Blueberries	——
Strawberries	——	Bananas	——	Bananas	——

Practice

Write fractions to match the waffle toppings.

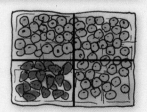

Blueberries ☐ ——

Strawberries ☐ ——

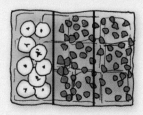

Bananas ☐ ——

Chocolate Chips ☐ ——

Chocolate Chips 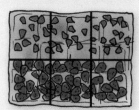 ——

Strawberries ☐ ——

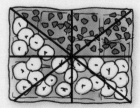

Bananas ☐ ——

Chocolate Chips ☐ ——

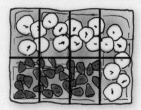

Strawberries ☐ ——

Bananas ☐ ——

Strawberries ☐ ——

Bananas ☐ ——

Review

Match pairs that equal 1,000.

| 800 | 700 | 600 | 750 | 650 |

| 300 | 250 | 200 | 350 | 400 |

Complete.

4 × 6 = ☐   7 × 2 = ☐   5 × 8 = ☐

3 × 3 = ☐   8 × 3 = ☐   1 × 6 = ☐

5 × 7 = ☐   2 × 9 = ☐   3 × 7 = ☐

0 × 6 = ☐   6 × 5 = ☐   4 × 4 = ☐

8 × 2 = ☐   7 × 4 = ☐   9 × 3 = ☐

Round to the nearest hundred.

895	
536	
450	
707	
619	
244	

Copy the shapes.

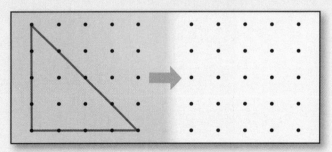

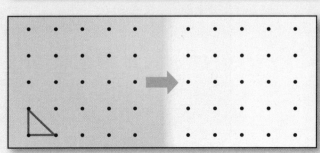

Lesson Activities 👥

A

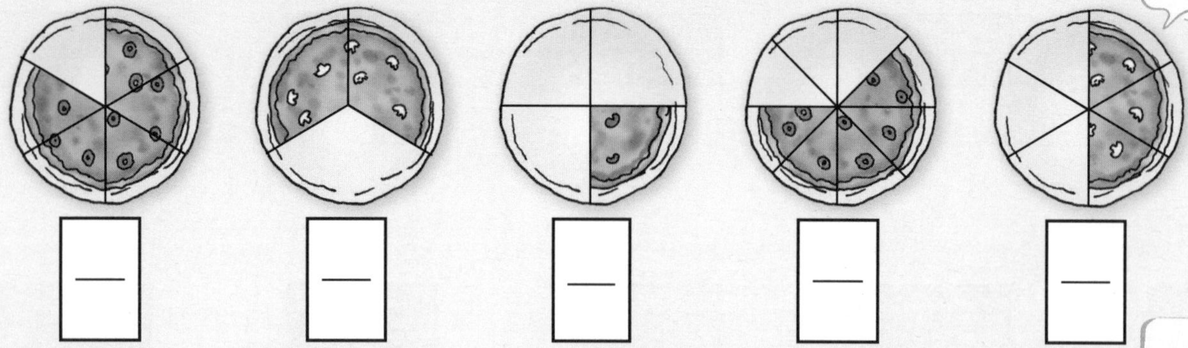

B

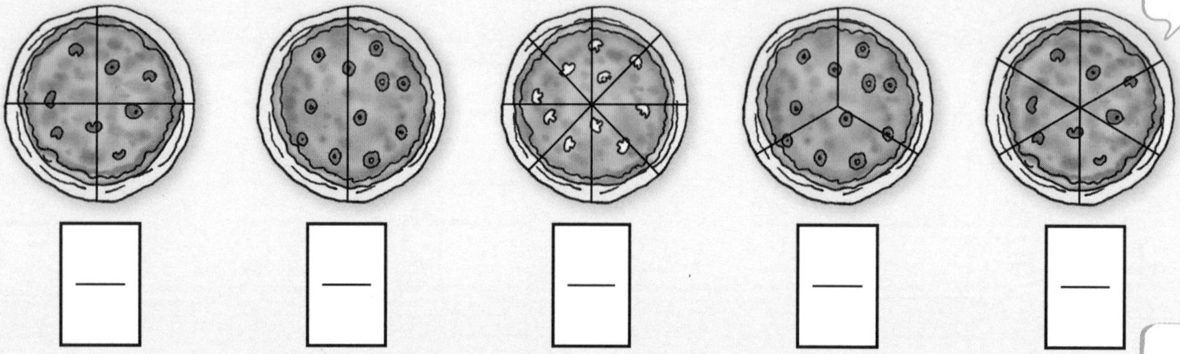

C

Fraction Four in a Row

$\frac{5}{8}$	$\frac{7}{8}$	$\frac{0}{8}$	$\frac{1}{2}$	$\frac{1}{4}$
$\frac{2}{8}$	$\frac{5}{6}$	$\frac{4}{6}$	$\frac{2}{3}$	$\frac{3}{6}$
$\frac{3}{6}$	$\frac{2}{4}$	$\frac{3}{8}$	$\frac{4}{4}$	$\frac{1}{6}$
$\frac{1}{3}$	$\frac{8}{8}$	$\frac{1}{2}$	$\frac{6}{8}$	$\frac{2}{6}$
$\frac{3}{4}$	$\frac{5}{6}$	$\frac{0}{4}$	$\frac{2}{4}$	$\frac{1}{8}$

Practice 👤 Complete the fractions to match the toppings.

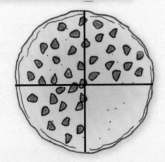
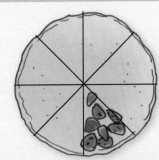
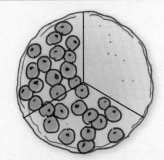

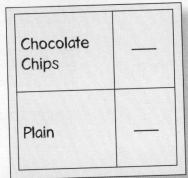

Chocolate Chips	—
Plain	—

Strawberries	—
Plain	—

Blueberries	—
Plain	—

Match pairs of fractions that equal one whole.

Solve.

Gabe's family ate $\frac{3}{8}$ of this pie.

What fraction of the pie did they have left?

Aria put strawberries on $\frac{1}{6}$ of her waffle.

She left the rest plain.

What fraction of the waffle was plain?

6.3

Review 👤 Match.

4 × 7	28	3 × 8	18
4 × 10	36	3 × 9	30
4 × 9	24	3 × 7	24
4 × 6	40	3 × 10	27
4 × 8	32	3 × 6	21

Complete.

5 × 30 = ☐

4 × 20 = ☐

2 × 30 = ☐

2 × 35 = ☐

Write the time.

[:]   [:]

Solve. Write the equations you use.

Samuel's bookshelf has 3 shelves.
There are 9 books on each shelf.
How many books are on the bookshelf?

Samuel's book has 319 pages.
He has already read 184 pages.
How many pages does he have left to read?

Lesson Activities

A

1 apple + 2 apples = ☐ apples

1 fourth + 2 fourths = ☐ fourths

$\dfrac{1}{4} + \dfrac{2}{4} = \dfrac{}{}$

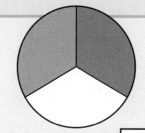

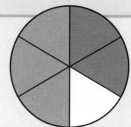

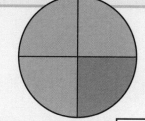

$\dfrac{1}{3} + \dfrac{1}{3} = \dfrac{}{}$

$\dfrac{3}{6} + \dfrac{2}{6} = \dfrac{}{}$

$\dfrac{3}{4} + \dfrac{1}{4} = \dfrac{}{}$

B

SPIN A PIZZA

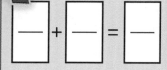
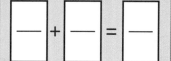

Player 1	Player 2
☐ + ☐ = ☐	☐ + ☐ = ☐
☐ + ☐ = ☐	☐ + ☐ = ☐
☐ + ☐ = ☐	☐ + ☐ = ☐
☐ + ☐ = ☐	☐ + ☐ = ☐
☐ + ☐ = ☐	☐ + ☐ = ☐

Practice 👤 Complete.

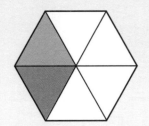

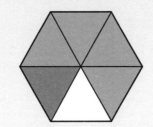

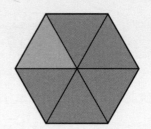

$\frac{1}{6} + \frac{1}{6} = \boxed{\frac{}{}}$ $\frac{4}{6} + \frac{1}{6} = \boxed{\frac{}{}}$ ★ $\frac{1}{6} + \boxed{\frac{}{}} = \frac{6}{6}$

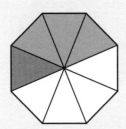

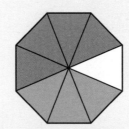

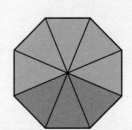

$\frac{1}{8} + \frac{3}{8} = \boxed{\frac{}{}}$ $\frac{4}{8} + \frac{3}{8} = \boxed{\frac{}{}}$ ★ $\frac{5}{8} + \boxed{\frac{}{}} = \frac{8}{8}$

Solve. Write an equation to match.

Henry ate $\frac{1}{8}$ of a pizza.

Then, he ate $\frac{2}{8}$ of the pizza.

What fraction of the pizza did he eat?

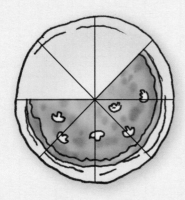

$\boxed{\frac{}{}} + \boxed{\frac{}{}} = \boxed{\frac{}{}}$

Elizabeth put green frosting on $\frac{2}{6}$ of the cake.

She put blue frosting on $\frac{3}{6}$ of the cake.

She left the rest plain.

What fraction of the cake has frosting?

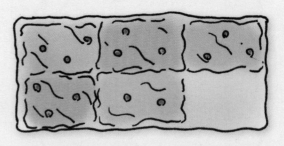

$\boxed{\frac{}{}} + \boxed{\frac{}{}} = \boxed{\frac{}{}}$

Review

Complete.

$2 \times 27 =$ ☐

$2 \times 25 =$ ☐

$2 \times 20 =$ ☐

$2 \times 48 =$ ☐

$2 \times 43 =$ ☐

$2 \times 40 =$ ☐

$7 \times 30 =$ ☐

$6 \times 30 =$ ☐

$5 \times 30 =$ ☐

⭐ $5 \times 41 =$ ☐

$5 \times 40 =$ ☐

$4 \times 40 =$ ☐

Aaron made a pictograph about raking leaves.
Use the pictograph to complete the chart and answer the questions.

Time Spent Raking Leaves

Wednesday | 🐾 🐾 🐾 🐾

Thursday | 🐾 🐾 🐾

Friday | 🐾 🐾 🐾 🐾 🐾 🐾

🐾 = 5 minutes

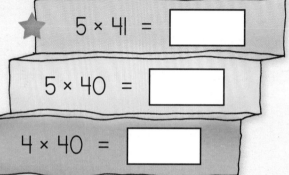

Day	Minutes
Wed.	
Thur.	
Fri.	

How much more time did he spend raking leaves on Friday than Thursday?

How much time did he spend raking leaves in all?

6.5

Lesson Activities 👥

A

3 apples – 1 apple = ☐ apples

3 fourths – 1 fourth = ☐ fourths

$\frac{3}{4} - \frac{1}{4} = \frac{}{}$

$\frac{5}{8} - \frac{3}{8} = \frac{}{}$

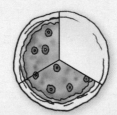

$\frac{2}{3} - \frac{1}{3} = \frac{}{}$

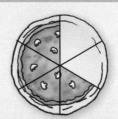

$\frac{4}{6} - \frac{2}{6} = \frac{}{}$

B

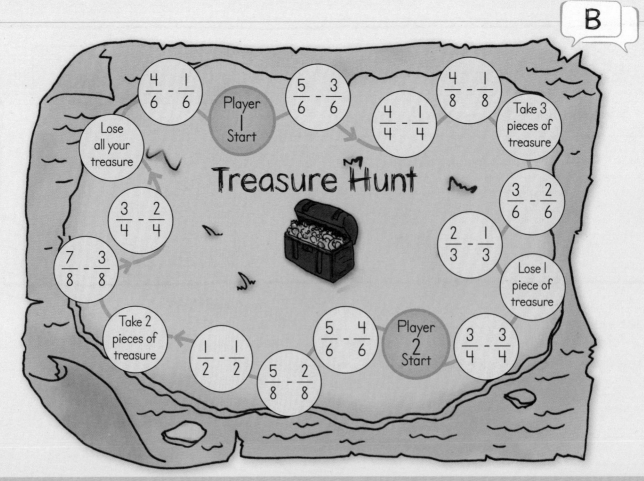

Treasure Hunt

Practice 👤 Complete. X out the pizza slices to match each equation.

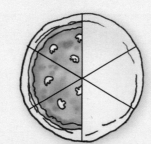
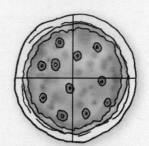

$\frac{5}{8} - \frac{2}{8} = \boxed{\ }$ $\frac{3}{6} - \frac{1}{6} = \boxed{\ }$ ⭐ $\frac{4}{4} - \frac{1}{4} = \boxed{\ }$

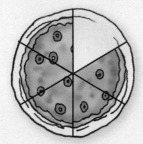
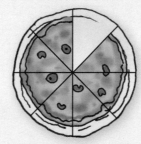
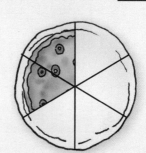

$\frac{5}{6} - \frac{4}{6} = \boxed{\ }$ $\frac{7}{8} - \frac{4}{8} = \boxed{\ }$ ⭐ $\frac{2}{6} - \frac{0}{6} = \boxed{\ }$

Solve. Write an equation to mach.

Hudson's family has $\frac{7}{8}$ of a pan of brownies. They eat $\frac{5}{8}$ of the pan. What fraction of the pan is left?

Bella's family has $\frac{5}{8}$ of a pizza. Bella eats $\frac{2}{8}$ of the pizza. What fraction of the whole pizza is left?

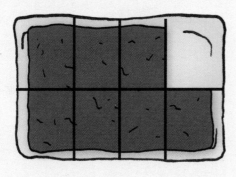
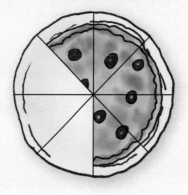

$\boxed{\ } - \boxed{\ } = \boxed{\ }$ $\boxed{\ } - \boxed{\ } = \boxed{\ }$

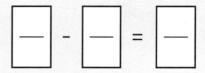

Review 👤 Complete.

×	1	2	3	4	5	6	7	8	9	10
1	1	2	3	4	5	6	7	8	9	10
2	2	4	6	8	10	12	14	16	18	20
3	3	6	9	12		18		24		30
4	4	8	12	16	20		28		36	40
5	5	10		20	25	30	35	40	45	50
6	6	12	18		30	36	42	48	54	60
7	7	14		28	35	42	49	56	63	70
8	8	16	24		40	48	56	64	72	80
9	9	18		36	45	54	63	72	81	90
10	10	20	30	40	50	60	70	80	90	100

Complete.

1 foot = ⬜ inches

1 yard = ⬜ feet

1 yard = ⬜ inches

1 meter = ⬜ centimeters

1 minute = ⬜ seconds

1 hour = ⬜ minutes

1 day = ⬜ hours

1 week = ⬜ days

Use a ruler to measure the sticks.

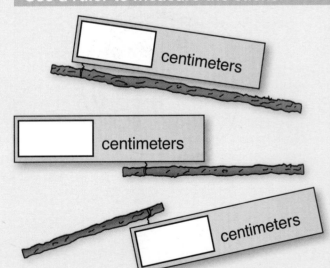

⬜ centimeters

⬜ centimeters

⬜ centimeters

Write each number in its expanded form.

396 = 300 + 90 + 6

475 = ⬜

808 = ⬜

880 = ⬜

Lesson Activities 👥

Multiplication Crash (×4)

| 12 | 24 | 36 | 8 | 40 |
| 28 | 4 | 32 | 20 | 16 |

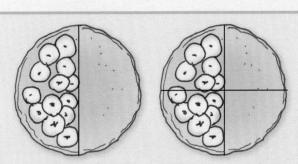

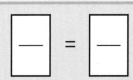
 B

□ = □

Equivalent Fractions
have the same value but have different numerators and denominators.

□ = □

  □ = □

□ = □

 □ = □

Practice

Complete the equivalent fractions to match the pancakes.

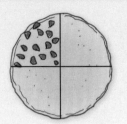 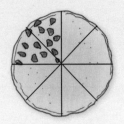

 =

 =

 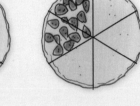

 =

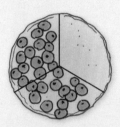 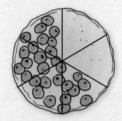

 =

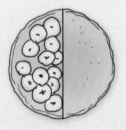 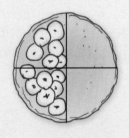 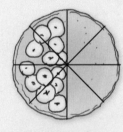 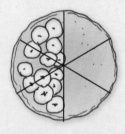

 = = =

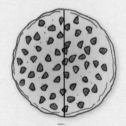 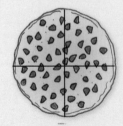 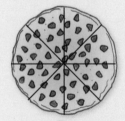 

 = = =

Review   Complete the fractions to match the pictures.

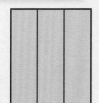

I whole = ▭

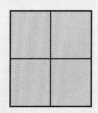

I whole = ▭

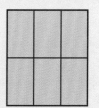

I whole = ▭

Complete.

	5
×	7

	8
×	3

	7
×	4

	4
×	1

	3
×	3

	3
×	9

	5
×	5

	4
×	2

	3
×	4

	9
×	4

Complete.

70 − 38 = ▭

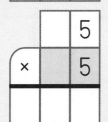 380 + 130 = ▭

70 − 18 = ▭

380 + 30 = ▭

70 − 8   = ▭

380 + 20 = ▭

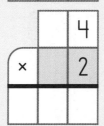 410 − 150 = ▭

2 × 36 = ▭

410 − 50 = ▭

2 × 33 = ▭

410 − 10 = ▭

2 × 30 = ▭

Lesson Activities

A

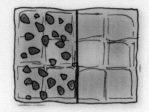 $\dfrac{1}{2} = \boxed{}$

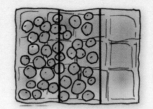 $\dfrac{2}{3} = \boxed{}$

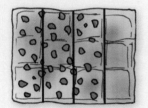 $\dfrac{3}{4} = \boxed{}$

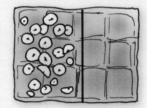 $\dfrac{1}{2} = \boxed{}$

B

Roll and Cover

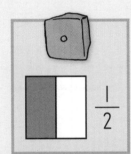 $\dfrac{1}{2}$ 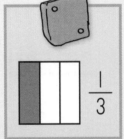 $\dfrac{1}{3}$ 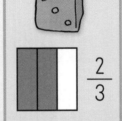 $\dfrac{2}{3}$ 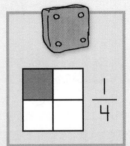 $\dfrac{1}{4}$ 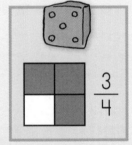 $\dfrac{3}{4}$

Player 1

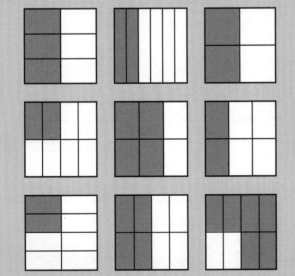

Player 2

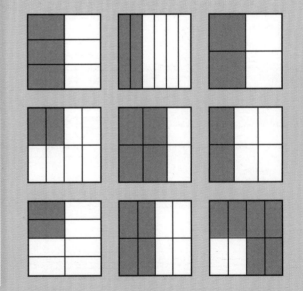

Practice

Color the second shape in each pair to match the first shape. Then, complete the fraction.

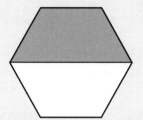

 $\frac{1}{2} = \frac{3}{6}$

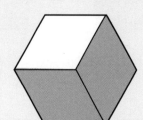 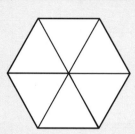

$\frac{2}{3} = \frac{}{}$

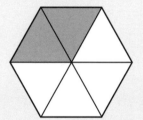 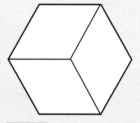

$\frac{2}{6} = \frac{}{}$

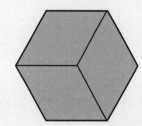 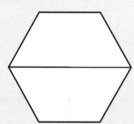

$\frac{3}{3} = \frac{}{}$

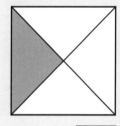 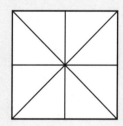

$\frac{1}{4} = \frac{}{}$

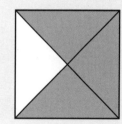 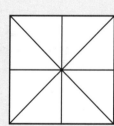

$\frac{3}{4} = \frac{}{}$

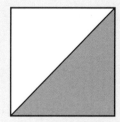 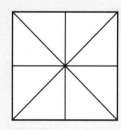

$\frac{1}{2} = \frac{}{}$

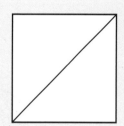 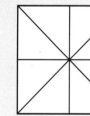

 $\frac{0}{2} = \frac{}{}$

6.7

Review 👤 Match pairs that equal 1,000.

| 860 | 560 | 760 | 460 | 660 |

| 240 | 140 | 440 | 340 | 540 |

Complete.

```
  4 3 8
+ 3 7 9
-------
```

```
  4 3 8
- 3 7 9
-------
```

Complete.

$300 + \boxed{} = 330$

$600 - \boxed{} = 400$

$\boxed{} + 75 = 575$

$\boxed{} - 200 = 500$

$\boxed{} - 1 = 399$

Solve. Write the equations you use.

Makayla had $32. She earned $18.
Then, she spent $9.
How much money did she have left?

Makayla jumped rope for 16 minutes on Friday, 27 minutes on Saturday, and 8 minutes on Sunday. How many minutes did she jump rope in all?

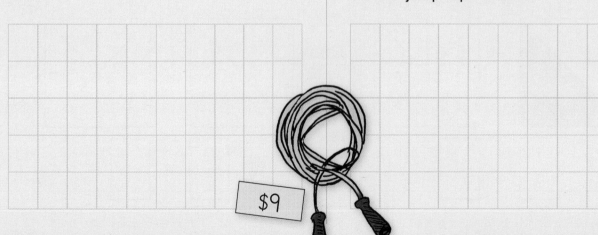

$9

Lesson Activities 👥

A

$\dfrac{1}{3}$ ◯ $\dfrac{2}{3}$

$\dfrac{3}{4}$ ◯ $\dfrac{1}{4}$

$\dfrac{1}{8}$ ◯ $\dfrac{5}{8}$ $\dfrac{3}{6}$ ◯ $\dfrac{2}{6}$ $\dfrac{3}{6}$ ◯ $\dfrac{1}{6}$

B

$\dfrac{}{}$ $\dfrac{}{}$ $\dfrac{}{}$ $\dfrac{}{}$ $\dfrac{}{}$

$\dfrac{1}{2}$ ◯ $\dfrac{1}{8}$ $\dfrac{1}{4}$ ◯ $\dfrac{1}{3}$ $\dfrac{1}{6}$ ◯ $\dfrac{1}{8}$

C

$\dfrac{1}{8}$ ◯ $\dfrac{1}{3}$ $\dfrac{1}{4}$ ◯ $\dfrac{1}{6}$ $\dfrac{1}{6}$ ◯ $\dfrac{1}{8}$

$\dfrac{2}{8}$ ◯ $\dfrac{2}{3}$ $\dfrac{2}{4}$ ◯ $\dfrac{2}{6}$ $\dfrac{3}{6}$ ◯ $\dfrac{3}{8}$

$\dfrac{3}{8}$ ◯ $\dfrac{3}{3}$ $\dfrac{3}{4}$ ◯ $\dfrac{3}{6}$ $\dfrac{5}{6}$ ◯ $\dfrac{5}{8}$

6.8

6.8

Practice 👤 **Write <, >, or =. Use the pictures to help.**

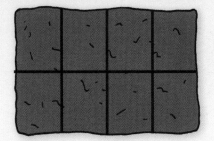
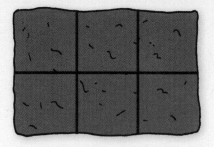

$\frac{2}{8}$ ◯ $\frac{5}{8}$ $\frac{3}{6}$ ◯ $\frac{1}{6}$

$\frac{3}{8}$ ◯ $\frac{7}{8}$ $\frac{4}{6}$ ◯ $\frac{5}{6}$

$\frac{8}{8}$ ◯ $\frac{4}{8}$ $\frac{2}{6}$ ◯ $\frac{2}{6}$

$\frac{1}{8}$ ◯ $\frac{6}{8}$ $\frac{6}{6}$ ◯ $\frac{5}{6}$

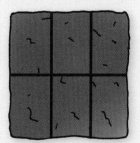

$\frac{1}{3}$ ◯ $\frac{1}{4}$ $\frac{1}{6}$ ◯ $\frac{1}{3}$

$\frac{2}{3}$ ◯ $\frac{2}{4}$ $\frac{2}{6}$ ◯ $\frac{2}{3}$

$\frac{3}{3}$ ◯ $\frac{3}{4}$ $\frac{3}{6}$ ◯ $\frac{3}{3}$

$\frac{3}{3}$ ◯ $\frac{4}{4}$ $\frac{6}{6}$ ◯ $\frac{3}{3}$

Review

Complete.

		3
×		6

		4
×		9

		5
×		5

		4
×		8

		7
×		1

		4
×		7

		3
×		8

		6
×		2

		9
×		5

	1	0
×		9

Complete.

$$\frac{3}{8} + \frac{3}{8} = \boxed{}$$

$$\frac{7}{8} - \frac{1}{8} = \boxed{}$$

$$\frac{3}{6} + \frac{1}{6} = \boxed{}$$

$$\frac{3}{4} - \frac{1}{4} = \boxed{}$$

Complete.

	4	5	9
+	1	8	6

	3	0	7
-	1	7	4

Complete.

$ \boxed{}$

$ \boxed{}$

6.9

Lesson Activities 👥

Less than $\frac{1}{2}$	Equal to $\frac{1}{2}$	Greater than $\frac{1}{2}$

$\frac{2}{6}$ $\frac{3}{6}$ $\frac{7}{8}$ $\frac{2}{3}$ $\frac{1}{4}$ $\frac{1}{8}$ $\frac{3}{4}$ $\frac{5}{6}$

$\frac{4}{6}$ $\frac{4}{8}$ $\frac{1}{3}$ $\frac{6}{8}$ $\frac{2}{4}$ $\frac{3}{8}$ $\frac{1}{6}$ $\frac{5}{8}$

B

$\frac{5}{8} \bigcirc \frac{1}{3}$ $\frac{3}{6} \bigcirc \frac{4}{8}$

$\frac{1}{3} \bigcirc \frac{3}{4}$ $\frac{1}{8} \bigcirc \frac{3}{6}$

$\frac{2}{4} \bigcirc \frac{5}{8}$ $\frac{5}{6} \bigcirc \frac{3}{8}$

Practice

Write fractions to match each shape.
Then, write the fractions in order from least to greatest.

LEAST ➡   ⬅ GREATEST

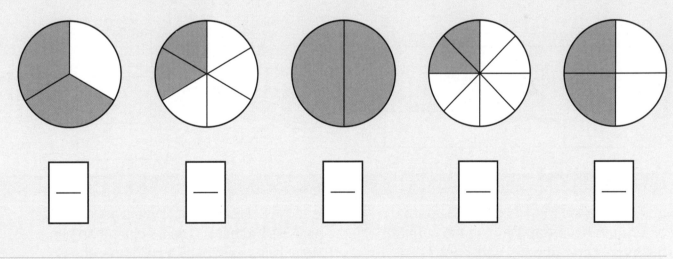

LEAST ➡   ⬅ GREATEST

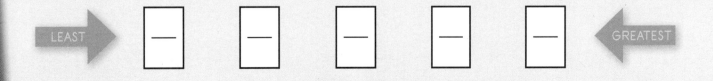

Review 👤 Complete.

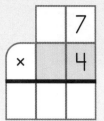

	7
×	4

	9
×	3

	3
×	4

	5
×	6

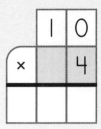

	1 0
×	4

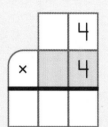

	4
×	4

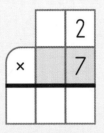

	2
×	7

	9
×	4

	8
×	3

	3
×	7

Write each money amount two ways.

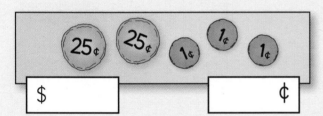

$ [   ]   [   ] ¢

$ [   ]   [   ] ¢

Complete.

$10 \times 10 =$ [   ]

$16 \times 10 =$ [   ]

$18 \times 10 =$ [   ]

$3 \times 50 =$ [   ]

$4 \times 30 =$ [   ]

$6 \times 20 =$ [   ]

Solve. Write the equations you use.

Isaac's mom is 35. His dad is 3 years older than his mom. What is the sum of his mom's age and his dad's age?

Isaac is 8. His sister is 2 years younger than him. His brother is 3 years older than him. What is the sum of all 3 children's ages?

Lesson Activities 👥

A

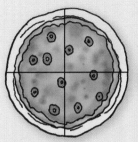 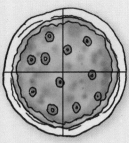 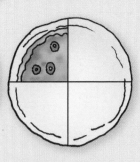

☐   ☐   Mixed Number

B

PUMPKIN BREAD INGREDIENTS

$1\frac{1}{3}$ cups sugar

$1\frac{1}{4}$ cups canned pumpkin puree

$\frac{3}{4}$ cup vegetable oil

$1\frac{1}{2}$ cups flour

$\frac{1}{2}$ cup chocolate chips

$\frac{2}{3}$ cup chopped walnuts

6.10

Practice 👤 **Write a mixed number to match each picture.**

☐ —

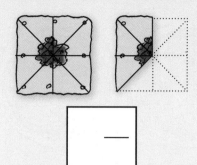

☐ —

☐ —

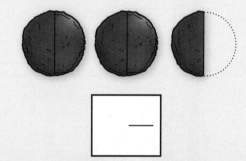

☐ —

☐ —

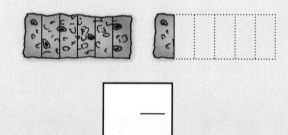

☐ —

Solve.

Oliver's dad has 3 pizzas.
He cuts each pizza into eighths.
How many slices does he get?

☐ slices

⭐ Jenna's mom has 2 cakes. She wants
to serve the cakes to 12 people.
What fractional part should she cut
each cake into?

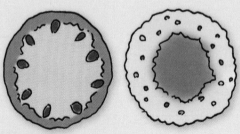

She should cut
each cake into ☐ .

Review  Complete the equivalent fractions.

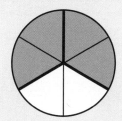
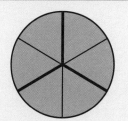

$\frac{1}{3} = \frac{\boxed{}}{6}$ $\frac{2}{3} = \frac{\boxed{}}{6}$ $\frac{3}{3} = \frac{\boxed{}}{6}$

Complete.

$10 \times 4 = \boxed{}$ $7 \times 3 = \boxed{}$ $5 \times 4 = \boxed{}$

$2 \times 3 = \boxed{}$ $4 \times 6 = \boxed{}$ $3 \times 6 = \boxed{}$

$8 \times 4 = \boxed{}$ $1 \times 3 = \boxed{}$ $4 \times 4 = \boxed{}$

$4 \times 3 = \boxed{}$ $3 \times 5 = \boxed{}$ $3 \times 10 = \boxed{}$

Solve. Write the equations you use.

The game costs $27.
Hazel gives the clerk $40.
How much change does she get?

Hazel scored 285 points in the game.
Lauren scored 315 points.
How many more points did Lauren
score than Hazel?

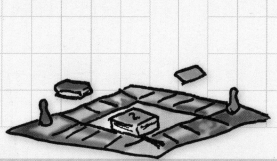

Unit Wrap-Up

Use the words in the word bank to complete the blanks.

| equivalent fractions | ○ | denominator | ○ | mixed numbers | ○ | numerator |

$\frac{1}{3}$

The top number is the _____.
It tells how many parts.

The bottom number is the _____.
It tells how many equal parts the whole was split into.

$\frac{1}{3}$ = $\frac{2}{6}$

Fractions that look different but have the same value are called _____.

$2\frac{1}{2}$

Numbers with a whole number and a fraction are called _____.

Use the key to color the fractions.

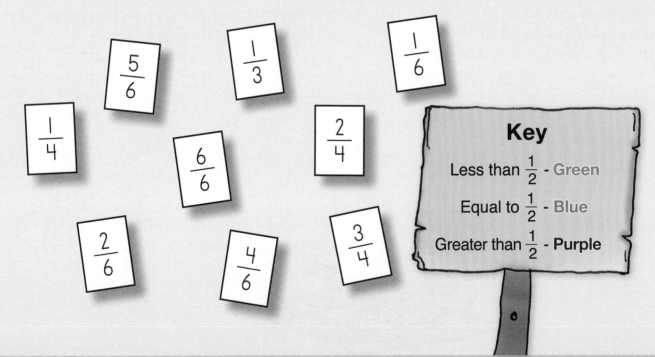

$\frac{5}{6}$ $\frac{1}{3}$ $\frac{1}{6}$

$\frac{1}{4}$ $\frac{6}{6}$ $\frac{2}{4}$

$\frac{2}{6}$ $\frac{4}{6}$ $\frac{3}{4}$

Key

Less than $\frac{1}{2}$ - Green

Equal to $\frac{1}{2}$ - Blue

Greater than $\frac{1}{2}$ - Purple

Unit Wrap-Up

Write <, >, or =.

$$\frac{1}{6} \bigcirc \frac{4}{6}$$

$$\frac{1}{4} \bigcirc \frac{1}{8}$$

$$\frac{3}{8} \bigcirc \frac{3}{4}$$

$$\frac{7}{8} \bigcirc \frac{1}{6}$$

Complete.

$$\frac{5}{6} - \frac{2}{6} = \boxed{\frac{}{}}$$

$$\frac{3}{8} + \frac{4}{8} = \boxed{\frac{}{}}$$

$$\frac{8}{8} - \frac{1}{8} = \boxed{\frac{}{}}$$

$$\frac{7}{8} + \frac{1}{8} = \boxed{\frac{}{}}$$

Complete the equivalent fractions.

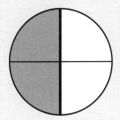

$$\frac{1}{2} = \boxed{\frac{}{4}}$$

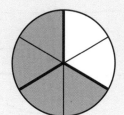

$$\frac{2}{3} = \boxed{\frac{}{6}}$$

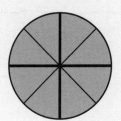

$$\frac{4}{4} = \boxed{\frac{}{8}}$$

Write a mixed number to match each picture.

$$\boxed{\frac{}{}}$$

$$\boxed{\frac{}{}}$$

Lesson Activities 👥

A

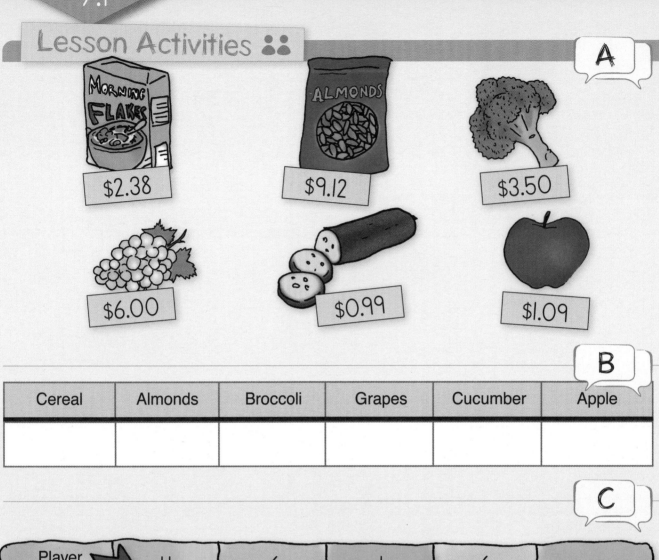

MORNING FLAKES $2.38

ALMONDS $9.12

$3.50

$6.00

$0.99

$1.09

B

Cereal	Almonds	Broccoli	Grapes	Cucumber	Apple

C

Race to $10.00

Player 1 START	4 pennies	6 dimes	1 dollar	6 pennies	5 dimes
3 dollars					2 dollars
7 dimes					8 pennies
9 pennies					3 dimes
2 dollars					3 dollars
5 dimes	7 pennies	1 dollar	4 dimes	5 pennies	Player 2 START

Practice 👤 **Round each price to the nearest dollar.**

$2.09	$2.19	$2.49	$2.59	$2.79	$2.89
$2					

$3.17	$6.94	$8.50	$12.64	$38.07	$46.39

Complete with <, >, or =.

$2.47 ◯ $2.74

$2.40 ◯ $2.04

$2.00 ◯ $2

$0.02 ◯ $0.20

$2.02 ◯ $2.00

Complete. Use a dollar sign and decimal point for each amount.

Coins	Value
4 pennies	$
4 nickels	
4 dimes	
4 quarters	

Solve.

Gabe has 4 dimes and 6 pennies.
Sarah has 3 dimes and 3 nickels.
Who has more money? How much more?

Gisele has 3 quarters.
Eli has 5 dimes, 4 nickels, and 2 pennies.
Who has more money? How much more?

7.1

Review 👤   Write mixed numbers to match the shapes.

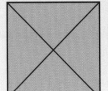 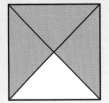   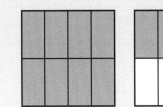

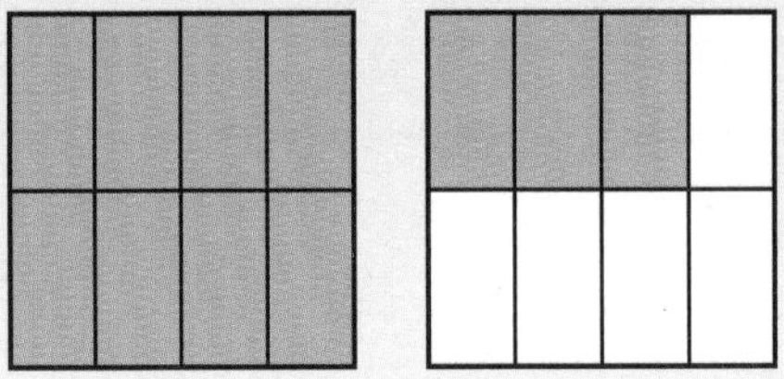

Complete.

36   +6 → ⬜   +6 → ⬜   +6 → ⬜   +6 → 60

42   +7 → ⬜   +7 → ⬜   +7 → ⬜   +7 → 70

48   +8 → ⬜   +8 → ⬜   +8 → ⬜   +8 → 80

Complete.

25 + 50 = ⬜

75 + 25 = ⬜

150 + 25 = ⬜

50 + 150 = ⬜

200 + 250 = ⬜

Match pairs that equal 100.

38   72

48   82

28   52

18   62

Lesson Activities 👥

214 ¢ = $ [   ]

139 ¢ = $ [   ]   201 ¢ = $ [   ]

400 ¢ = $ [   ]   445 ¢ = $ [   ]

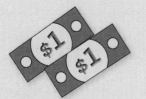

$ 2.25 = [   ] ¢

$ 3.50 = [   ] ¢ $ 3.79 = [   ] ¢

$ 5.00 = [   ] ¢ $ 5.07 = [   ] ¢

$ 0.80 + $ 0.40 = $ [   ] $ 1.30 − $ 0.60 = $ [   ]

80 ¢ + 40 ¢ = [   ] ¢   130 ¢ − 60 ¢ = [   ] ¢

Roll and Add

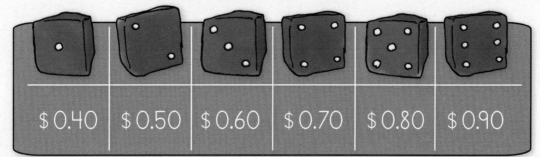

| $ 0.40 | $ 0.50 | $ 0.60 | $ 0.70 | $ 0.80 | $ 0.90 |

7.2

Practice 👤 Complete.

$	¢
$2.00	200 ¢
$2.09	
$2.45	
$2.50	
$2.99	

$	¢
	400 ¢
	406 ¢
	410 ¢
	432 ¢
	457 ¢

$	¢
$9.25	
$5.07	
	615 ¢
	891 ¢
$3.79	

Use the chart to solve.

Chips.........................$0.90
Pretzels $1.10
Crackers....................$1.00
Fruit Snacks $0.70
Granola Bar..............$0.80

How much does it cost to buy chips and a granola bar?

How much does it cost to buy fruit snacks and pretzels?

How much more do crackers cost than chips?

How much less does a granola bar cost than chips?

You buy fruit snacks. You give the clerk $1.00. How much change do you get?

 You buy pretzels. You give the clerk $2.00. How much change do you get?

Review 👤 Complete.

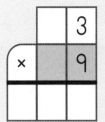

	3
×	9

	1	0
×	1	0

		9
×		5

		4
×		3

		2
×		9

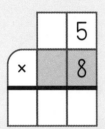
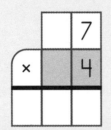
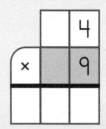

		5
×		8

		7
×		4

	1	0
×		7

		4
×		9

		1
×		8

Complete.

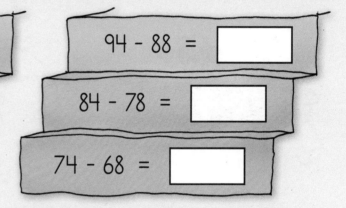

52 − 47 = [ ]

51 − 46 = [ ]

50 − 45 = [ ]

94 − 88 = [ ]

84 − 78 = [ ]

74 − 68 = [ ]

Solve.

You give the clerk $30.
How much change do you get?

$16

Change
$

You give the clerk $50.
How much change do you get?

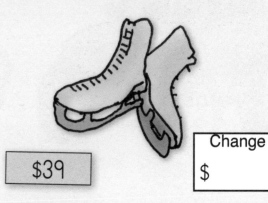

$39

Change
$

Lesson Activities 👥

A

You pay the clerk $9.
How much change do you get?

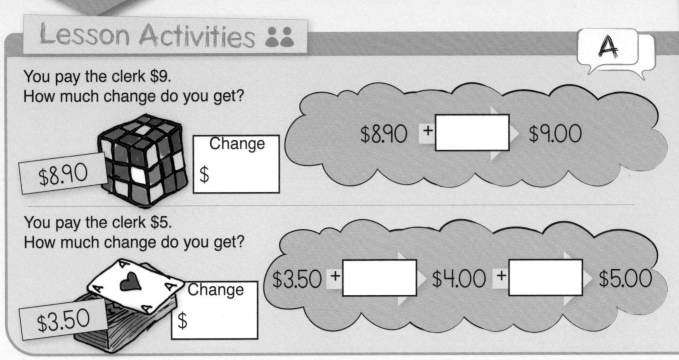

$8.90

Change
$

$8.90 + ☐ ➔ $9.00

You pay the clerk $5.
How much change do you get?

$3.50

Change
$

$3.50 + ☐ ➔ $4.00 + ☐ ➔ $5.00

B

Pretend Store

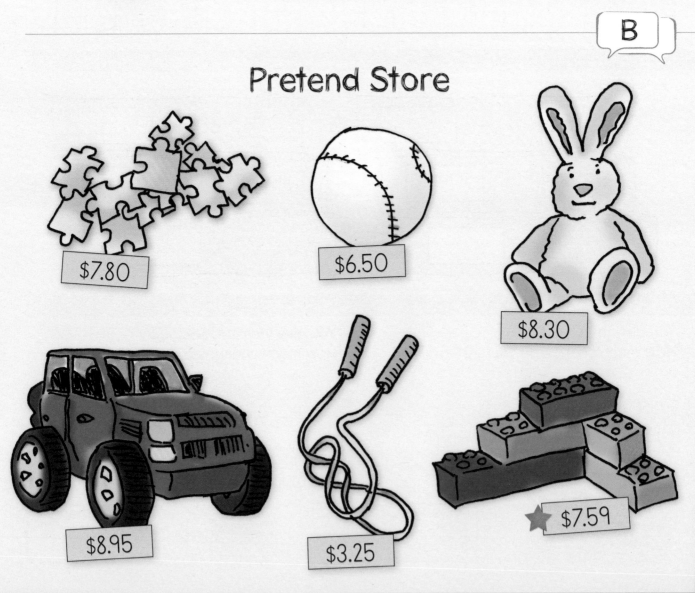

$7.80

$6.50

$8.30

$8.95

$3.25

★ $7.59

Practice 👤 Complete.

$2.80 + $ 0.20 = $3.00 $4.75 + $ _____ = $6.00

$3.40 + $ _____ = $4.00 $6.95 + $ _____ = $8.00

$5.75 + $ _____ = $10.00 $7.50 + $ _____ = $10.00

$6.70 + $ _____ = $10.00   ⭐ $3.79 + $ _____ = $10.00

Solve.

You pay the clerk $3.00.
How much change
do you get?

Change
$ _____

$2.35

You pay the clerk $5.00.
How much change
do you get?

Change
$ _____

$4.25

You pay the clerk $10.00.
How much change do you get?

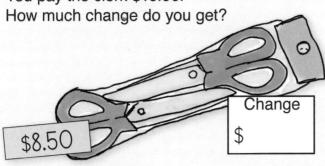

Change
$ _____

$8.50

⭐ You pay the clerk $20.00.
How much change do you get?

Change
$ _____

$16.49

Review 👤 Complete with <, >, or =.

$\frac{1}{8} \bigcirc \frac{1}{4}$ $\frac{2}{8} \bigcirc \frac{2}{4}$ $\frac{3}{8} \bigcirc \frac{3}{4}$

$\frac{8}{8} \bigcirc \frac{2}{4}$ $\frac{7}{8} \bigcirc \frac{1}{4}$ $\frac{4}{8} \bigcirc \frac{2}{4}$

Match.

4 × 7	32		3 × 8	24
3 × 6	18		4 × 9	27
4 × 8	28		8 × 5	36
3 × 7	24		3 × 9	40
4 × 6	21		9 × 5	45

Complete.

```
  4 8 6
+ 3 9 0
```

```
  6 4 0
- 1 7 3
```

Complete.

$1.50 = \boxed{}$ ¢

$2.96 = \boxed{}$ ¢

$5.74 = \boxed{}$ ¢

$\boxed{}$ = 174 ¢

$\boxed{}$ = 800 ¢

Lesson Activities 👥

A

YARD SALE!

$7.00

$1.40

$3.00

$3.90

$2.50

$4.30

$7.20

$0.70

$7.00 + $1.40 = ☐

$7.00 → +$1.00 → ☐ → +$0.40 → ☐

$3.90 + $4.30 = ☐

$3.90 → +$4.00 → ☐ → +$0.30 → ☐

Practice 👤 Complete.

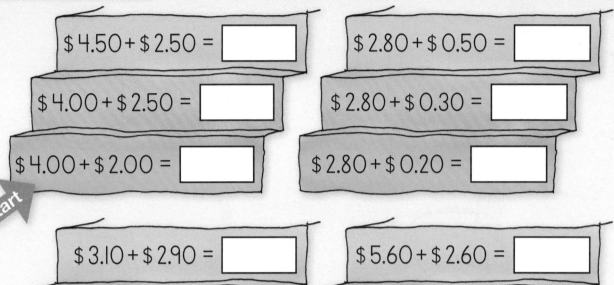

$4.50 + $2.50 = ☐ $2.80 + $0.50 = ☐

$4.00 + $2.50 = ☐ $2.80 + $0.30 = ☐

$4.00 + $2.00 = ☐ $2.80 + $0.20 = ☐

Start

$3.10 + $2.90 = ☐ $5.60 + $2.60 = ☐

$3.10 + $2.70 = ☐ $5.60 + $0.60 = ☐

$3.10 + $2.00 = ☐ $5.60 + $0.40 = ☐

Use the chart to solve.

How much does it cost for a pony ride and a ferris wheel ride?

Carnival Activities

Ferris Wheel Ride..............$3.50
Ring Toss Game................$2.80
Carousel Ride...................$4.10
Face Painting $6.50
Pony Ride.........................$5.00

How much does it cost to have your face painted and take a ferris wheel ride?

You go on the carousel ride and pay $5.00. How much change do you get?

Review

Round to the nearest dollar.

$7.05	$7.55	$7.50	$17.05	$17.55	$17.50

Complete.

$$\frac{3}{8} + \frac{2}{8} = \boxed{\frac{}{}}$$

$$\frac{7}{8} - \frac{5}{8} = \boxed{\frac{}{}}$$

$$\frac{4}{6} + \frac{2}{6} = \boxed{\frac{}{}}$$

$$\frac{6}{6} - \frac{6}{6} = \boxed{\frac{}{}}$$

Connect each number to its place on the number line.

898	901	903

890   900   910

899	902	904

Color the problems that match the number in the star.

100

10 × 10
2 × 50
3 × 30

150

2 × 60
3 × 50
5 × 30

200

10 × 20
2 × 100
4 × 40

Lesson Activities 👥

A

$6.00 - $2.00 = [   ] $7.50 - $4.00 = [   ]

$5.50 - $2.20 = [   ] $5.50 —$2.00 → [   ] —$0.20 → [   ]

$3.00 - $1.20 = [   ] $3.00 —$1.00 → [   ] —$0.20 → [   ]

⭐ $4.10 - $2.70 = [   ] $4.10 —$2.00 → [   ] —$0.70 → [   ]

B

Player 1 START	$1.60	$0.50	$1.00	$0.70	$1.70
$3.00					$2.00
$0.90					$1.50
$2.10					$2.20
$2.00					$3.00
$1.20	$2.50	$1.00	$1.40	$0.80	Player 2 START

Shopping Spree

Practice 👤 Complete.

$3.50 - $1.50 = ☐

⭐ $6.10 - $3.20 = ☐

$3.50 - $1.40 = ☐

$6.10 - $3.10 = ☐

Start ➤ $3.50 - $1.00 = ☐

$6.10 - $3.00 = ☐

$7.00 - $2.90 = ☐

$10.00 - $3.50 = ☐

$7.00 - $2.50 = ☐

$9.00 - $3.50 = ☐

$7.00 - $2.00 = ☐

$8.00 - $3.50 = ☐

Use the chart to solve.

How much less does a cookie cost than a pretzel?

Winter Festival Menu

Pretzel............................ $4.50
Hot Chocolate $1.75
Soup $5.25
Cookie......................... $2

You have $3. If you buy hot chocolate, how much money will you have left?

 You have $10.
You buy soup and a cookie.
How much money will you have left?

Review 👤 Write the time.

| : | | : | | : | | : |

Complete.

$5 \times 7 = \boxed{}$ $8 \times 4 = \boxed{}$ $5 \times 4 = \boxed{}$

$3 \times 5 = \boxed{}$ $0 \times 9 = \boxed{}$ $7 \times 3 = \boxed{}$

$4 \times 6 = \boxed{}$ $5 \times 6 = \boxed{}$ $2 \times 8 = \boxed{}$

$2 \times 5 = \boxed{}$ $8 \times 3 = \boxed{}$ $3 \times 6 = \boxed{}$

Solve. Write the equations you use.

Alana read two books.
One book had 128 pages.
The other book had 306 pages.
How many pages did she read in all?

Alana read two books. One book had 128 pages. The other book had 306 pages. How many more pages did the longer book have than the shorter book?

Lesson Activities 👥

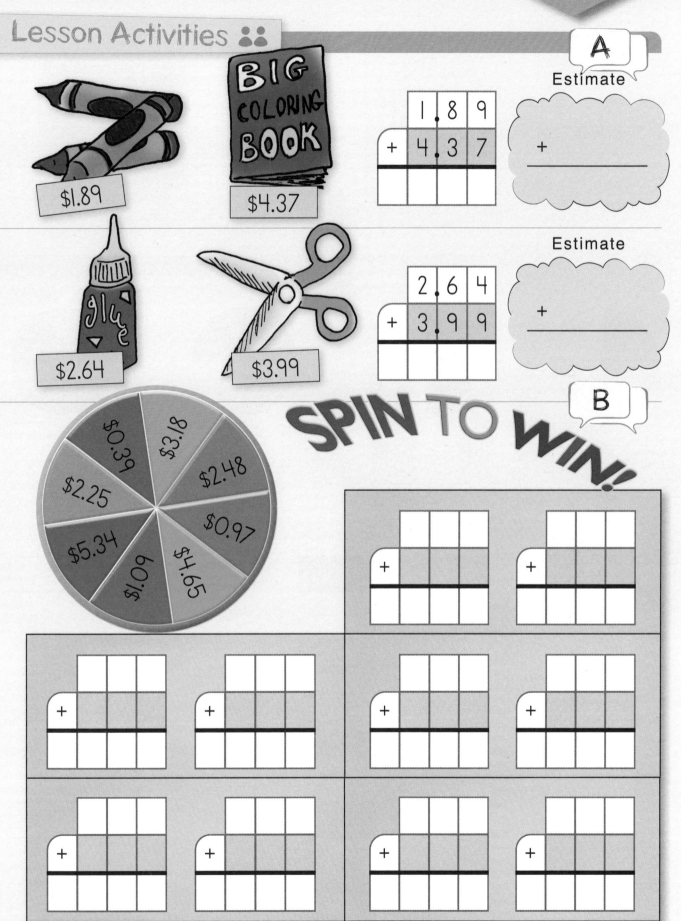

BIG COLORING BOOK

$1.89

$4.37

$2.64

$3.99

A

Estimate

	1	.	8	9
+	4	.	3	7

+ _____

Estimate

	2	.	6	4
+	3	.	9	9

+ _____

B

SPIN TO WIN!

Spinner values: $3.18, $2.48, $0.97, $4.65, $1.09, $5.34, $2.25, $0.39

7.6

Practice 👤 **Complete.**

| 3 . 5 6 |
| + 2 . 2 6 |

| 1 . 7 4 |
| + 2 . 4 3 |

| 4 . 3 8 |
| + 0 . 6 2 |

⭐ | 7 . 9 4 |
| + 8 . 6 7 |

Review 👤 **Complete the equivalent fractions.**

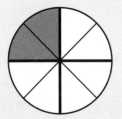
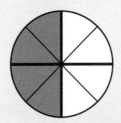
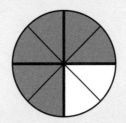
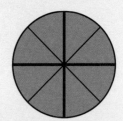

$\frac{1}{4} = \frac{}{8}$ $\frac{2}{4} = \frac{}{8}$ $\frac{3}{4} = \frac{}{8}$ $\frac{4}{4} = \frac{}{8}$

Match.

| 2 × 60 |

| 110 |

| 4 × 30 |

| 2 × 70 |

| 120 |

| 11 × 10 |

| 2 × 55 |

| 130 |

| 3 × 50 |

| 2 × 75 |

| 140 |

| 7 × 20 |

| 2 × 65 |

| 150 |

| 10 × 13 |

Lesson Activities 👥

A

Estimate

$3.45

	7	.	1	9
−		3	.	4	5

−
_____

Estimate

$6.32

	9	.	0	0
−		6	.	3	2

−
_____

B

GIFT CARD — THE CRAFTY STORE

BALANCE: $9.50

$1.68 $1.59 $2.17

$2.09 $2.36 $1.95

9	.	5	0
−			

Practice 👤 Complete.

| 7.7 7 |
| - 3.3 3 |
| |

| 8.9 0 |
| - 3.6 8 |
| |

| 4.3 8 |
| - 2.9 8 |
| |

| 6.0 0 |
| - 2.3 7 |
| |

Review 👤 Complete.

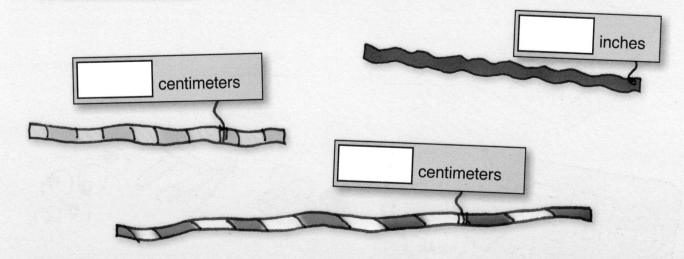

_____ inches

_____ centimeters

_____ centimeters

Jacob made a graph to show how much it snowed each month.
Use the graph to complete the chart.

Snowfall

Month	Inches of Snow
December	
January	
February	

Unit Wrap-Up 👤

Round to the nearest dollar.

$2.98	
$0.74	
$7.07	
$9.49	
$9.50	

Complete.

$	¢
$3.50	
	175 ¢
$4.07	
	316 ¢

Complete with <, >, or =.

56 pennies  ◯ $0.50

5 dimes ◯ $0.49

7 nickels ◯ $0.40

4 quarters ◯ $1.00

Match.

$3.00 + $1.80	$5.70	$6.90 − $1.40
$2.20 + $3.50	$4.50	$5.70 − $1.70
$2.40 + $1.60	$4.80	$7.00 − $2.20
$3.90 + $0.60	$5.50	$6.50 − $0.80
$3.90 + $1.60	$4.00	$8.00 − $3.50

7.8

👤 **Use the chart to answer the questions.
Write the equations you use.**

Thelma's Bakery

Pie............................ $9.49
Large cake $8.57
Small cake................ $4.99
Cookie..................... $1.25
Cupcake.................. $2.86

How much does it cost to buy a cookie
and a cupcake?

How much less does a small cake cost than
a large cake?

You have $9.00. You buy a large cake.
How much money do you have left?

A loaf of bread costs $1.43 more than a
cupcake. How much does a loaf of bread cost?

You buy a pie. You give the clerk $10.
How much change do you get?

⭐ You have $25. Do you have enough to buy
a pie, large cake, and small cake?

Lesson Activities 👥

A

6 × 1 = ☐   6 × 6 = ☐

6 × 2 = ☐   6 × 7 = ☐

6 × 3 = ☐   6 × 8 = ☐

6 × 4 = ☐   6 × 9 = ☐

6 × 5 = ☐   6 × 10 = ☐

B

5 × 8 = ☐   6 × 8 = ☐

5 × 6 = ☐   6 × 6 = ☐   5 × 7 = ☐   6 × 7 = ☐

5 × 9 = ☐

6 × 9 = ☐

Tic-Tac-Toe Crash (×6)

6	12	18
24	30	36
42	48	54

Practice   Complete.

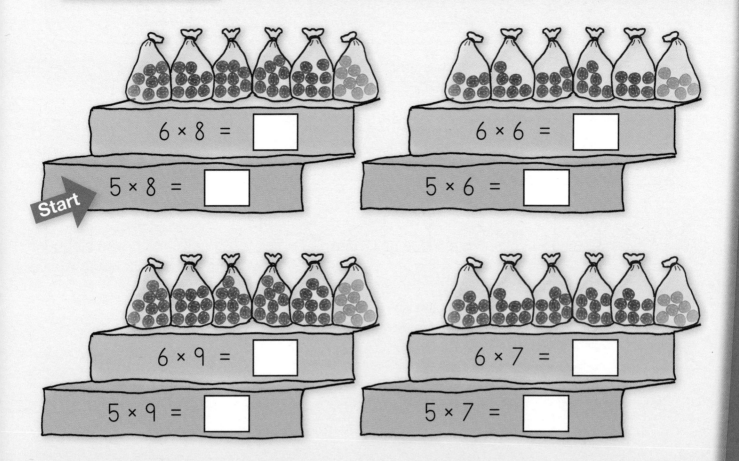

6 × 8 = ☐

6 × 6 = ☐

Start 5 × 8 = ☐

5 × 6 = ☐

6 × 9 = ☐

6 × 7 = ☐

5 × 9 = ☐

5 × 7 = ☐

Review

Complete.

35 + 7 = ☐

28 + 42 = ☐

36 + 36 = ☐

72 - 8 = ☐

81 - 45 = ☐

56 - 49 = ☐

Match.

$\frac{2}{2}$

$\frac{3}{3}$

$\frac{4}{4}$

$\frac{6}{6}$

$\frac{8}{8}$

Complete.

	4	.	9	0
-	2	.	4	8
$				

	6	.	7	5
-	3	.	4	0
$				

	8	.	1	0
-	3	.	1	2
$				

Solve. Write the equations you use to solve the problems.

Jerome has $7.50.
He spends $2.00 on a toy car.
Then, he spends $3.50 on a deck of cards.
How much money does he have left?

One day, Anna does 50 exercises.
She does 23 jumping jacks and 8 push-ups.
The rest of the exercises are sit-ups.
How many sit-ups does she do?

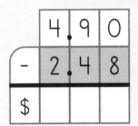

Lesson Activities 👥

5 × 7 = ☐   5 × 8 = ☐   5 × 9 = ☐

6 × 7 = ☐   6 × 8 = ☐   6 × 9 = ☐

Multiplication Bingo (×6)

B	I	N	G	O
42	36	60	6	24
36	18	12	48	30
6	60	42	54	48
48	54	30	60	42
24	36	54	18	12

B	I	N	G	O
36	24	6	18	30
6	48	12	60	42
12	24	36	54	18
54	30	18	48	60
6	42	30	12	24

C

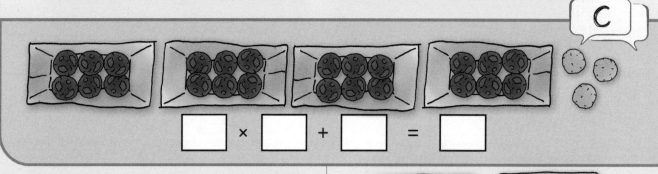

☐ × ☐ + ☐ = ☐

☐ × ☐ + ☐ = ☐   ☐ × ☐ + ☐ = ☐

Practice 👤 Complete.

		6
×		3

		6
×		8

		6
×		2

		6
×		9

		6
×		4

		6
×		7

		6
×		1

		6
×		6

		6
×		5

	1	0
×		6

Complete the equations to match the pictures.

□ × □ + □ = □

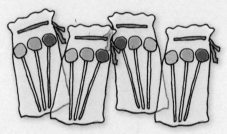 

□ × □ + □ = □

□ × □ + □ = □

□ × □ + □ = □

□ × □ + □ = □

□ × □ + □ = □

Review 👤 Complete.

$$\frac{7}{8} + \frac{1}{8} = \boxed{}$$

⭐ $$\frac{6}{8} + \boxed{\frac{}{8}} = \frac{8}{8}$$

$$\frac{5}{8} + \frac{3}{8} = \boxed{}$$

⭐ $$\frac{4}{8} + \boxed{\frac{}{8}} = \frac{8}{8}$$

Solve.

You pay the clerk $5.00.
How much change do you get?

$3.75

Change
$ [ ]

You pay the clerk $10.00.
How much change do you get?

$7.95

Change
$ [ ]

Write the time.

[:]

[:]

[:]

[:]

Complete.

5	.	3	2
+ 0	.	8	9
$			

8	.	3	2
− 0	.	8	9
$			

Lesson Activities

9 × 1 = [ ]   9 × 6 = [ ]

9 × 2 = [ ]   9 × 7 = [ ]

9 × 3 = [ ]   9 × 8 = [ ]

9 × 4 = [ ]   9 × 9 = [ ]

9 × 5 = [ ]   9 × 10 = [ ]

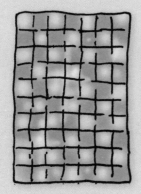

10 × 7 = [ ]

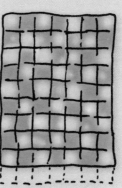

9 × 7 = [ ]

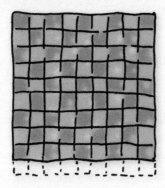

10 × 9 = [ ]

9 × 9 = [ ]

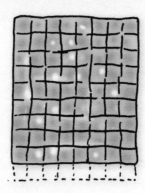

10 × 8 = [ ]

9 × 8 = [ ]

Multiplication Crash (×9)

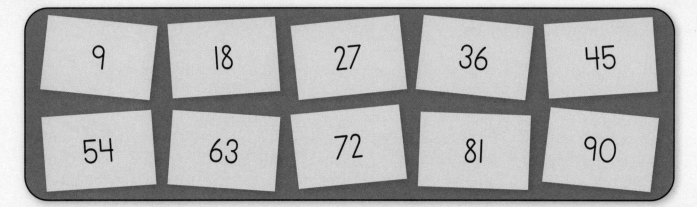

| 9 | 18 | 27 | 36 | 45 |
| 54 | 63 | 72 | 81 | 90 |

Practice 👤 Use the chart to answer the questions.
Write a multiplication equation for each question.

How much does bowling cost for 10 guests?

☐ × ☐ = $ ☐

BOWLING BIRTHDAY PARTY OPTIONS

Bowling $9
Pizza $8
Party favors $7

All prices are per guest.

How much does bowling cost for 9 guests?

☐ × ☐ = $ ☐

How much does pizza cost for 10 guests?

☐ × ☐ = $ ☐

How much do party favors cost for 10 guests?

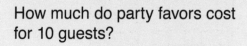

☐ × ☐ = $ ☐

How much does pizza cost for 9 guests?

☐ × ☐ = $ ☐

How much do party favors cost for 9 guests?

☐ × ☐ = $ ☐

Review Complete.

$$\frac{3}{4} - \frac{1}{4} = \boxed{}$$

⭐ $$\frac{2}{3} - \boxed{} = \frac{1}{3}$$

$$\frac{4}{4} - \frac{1}{4} = \boxed{}$$

⭐ $$\boxed{} - \frac{5}{8} = \frac{3}{8}$$

Complete.

	4	.	7	3
+	2	.	9	1
$				

	6	.	7	8
-	2	.	5	5
$				

	7	.	1	0
-	4	.	3	9
$				

Complete.

$6 \times 3 + 2 = \boxed{}$

$4 \times 4 + 1 = \boxed{}$

$9 \times 4 + 3 = \boxed{}$

$10 \times 6 + 5 = \boxed{}$

$8 \times 4 + 4 = \boxed{}$

Color the even numbers red.
Color the odd numbers yellow.

136 800 497 650 305 725 520

Lesson Activities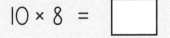

10 × 8 = ☐   10 × 7 = ☐   10 × 9 = ☐   **A**

9 × 8 = ☐   9 × 7 = ☐   9 × 9 = ☐

B

Climb and Slide

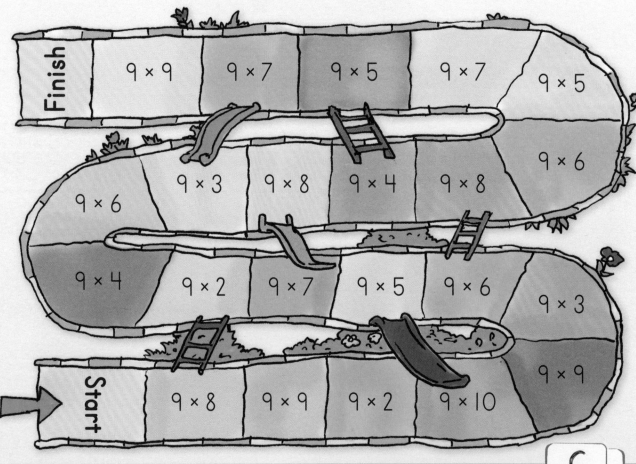

Finish | 9 × 9 | 9 × 7 | 9 × 5 | 9 × 7 | 9 × 5

9 × 6

9 × 6 | 9 × 3 | 9 × 8 | 9 × 4 | 9 × 8

9 × 4 | 9 × 2 | 9 × 7 | 9 × 5 | 9 × 6 | 9 × 3

9 × 9

Start | 9 × 8 | 9 × 9 | 9 × 2 | 9 × 10

C

Allie bought 6 packs of plain hair bows.
Each pack had 5 hair bows.
She also bought 2 fancy hair bows.
How many hair bows did she buy in all?

Tyler's parents bought tickets
to a play. They bought 4 adult tickets for
$10 each. They bought 3 child tickets for
$5 each. How much more did they spend
on adult tickets than child tickets?

Practice 👤 Color the multiples in order from Start to End.

Multiples of 9

Start → 9	3	20	64	75
18	27	36	42	90 **END**
12	24	45	72	81
15	48	54	63	56
8	16	30	60	35

Multiples of 6

25	20	32	63	60 **END**
16	27	28	56	54
12	18	24	45	48
Start → 6	20	30	36	42
4	16	32	40	45

Complete.

$9 \times 5 =$ ☐ $9 \times 9 =$ ☐ $9 \times 7 =$ ☐

$9 \times 10 =$ ☐ $9 \times 8 =$ ☐ $9 \times 6 =$ ☐

$6 \times 6 =$ ☐ $6 \times 10 =$ ☐ $6 \times 7 =$ ☐

$6 \times 9 =$ ☐ $6 \times 8 =$ ☐ $6 \times 5 =$ ☐

Solve. Write the equations you use.

Miriam bought 3 packs of large cups
and 2 packs of small cups for a party.
Each pack of large cups had 8 cups.
Each pack of small cups had 16 cups.
How many cups did she buy in all?

Micah bought 7 packs of trading cards.
Each pack had 4 cards.
He gave 5 of the cards to a friend.
How many cards did he have left?

Review 👤

Complete.

$3.50 + $2.20 = ☐

$6.80 + $1.30 = ☐

$3.50 + $3.50 = ☐

$4.00 - $1.00 = ☐

$4.00 - $1.50 = ☐

$4.00 - $2.50 = ☐

Complete with <, >, or =.

$\frac{8}{8}$ ◯ $\frac{6}{8}$

$\frac{1}{2}$ ◯ $\frac{5}{6}$

$\frac{2}{4}$ ◯ $\frac{3}{6}$

$\frac{1}{3}$ ◯ $\frac{1}{8}$

$\frac{0}{4}$ ◯ $\frac{0}{8}$

Draw a shape to match.

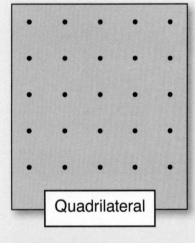
Quadrilateral

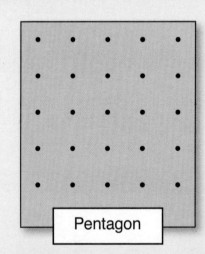
Pentagon

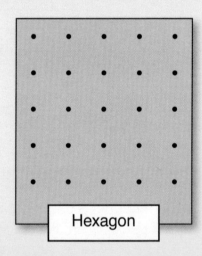
Hexagon

Use a ruler to draw a line that matches each length.

4 inches

10 centimeters

Lesson Activities

A

$8 × 1 =$ ☐ $8 × 6 =$ ☐

$8 × 2 =$ ☐ $8 × 7 =$ ☐

$8 × 3 =$ ☐ $8 × 8 =$ ☐

$8 × 4 =$ ☐ $8 × 9 =$ ☐

$8 × 5 =$ ☐ $8 × 10 =$ ☐

B

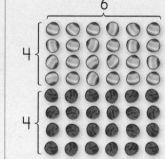

$4 × 8 =$ ☐

$8 × 8 =$ ☐

$4 × 7 =$ ☐

$8 × 7 =$ ☐

$4 × 6 =$ ☐

$8 × 6 =$ ☐

C

Multiplication Cover Up (×8)

Player 1	8	16	24	32	40	48	56	64	72	80

Player 2	8	16	24	32	40	48	56	64	72	80

Practice 👤 Complete.

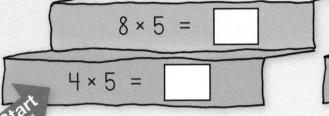

8 × 5 = [ ]

4 × 5 = [ ]

Start

8 × 6 = [ ]

4 × 6 = [ ]

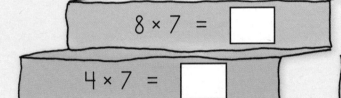

8 × 7 = [ ]

4 × 7 = [ ]

8 × 8 = [ ]

4 × 8 = [ ]

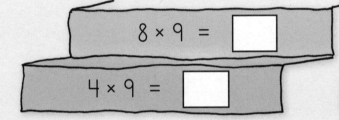 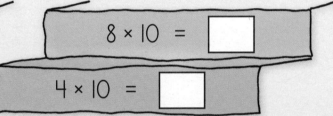

8 × 9 = [ ]

4 × 9 = [ ]

8 × 10 = [ ]

4 × 10 = [ ]

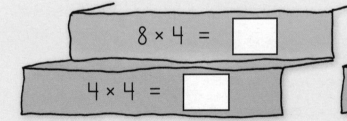 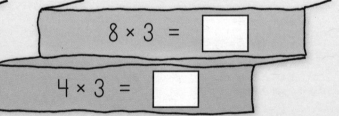

8 × 4 = [ ]

4 × 4 = [ ]

8 × 3 = [ ]

4 × 3 = [ ]

Solve. Write the equations you use to solve the problems.

Silas' family bought 6 packs of cupcakes for a party. Each pack had 8 cupcakes. How many cupcakes did they buy?

Alisha's family bought snacks for a party. They bought 3 bags of chips. Each bag cost $4. They bought 5 bottles of soda. Each bottle cost $2. How much did they spend?

Review 👤 **Draw lines to split each ribbon into the fractional part listed.**

Halves	Fourths	Eighths

Thirds	Sixths

Complete.

$6.05 = ☐ ¢

$3.25 = ☐ ¢

$4.97 = ☐ ¢

$ ☐ = 150 ¢

$ ☐ = 346 ¢

Complete.

1 foot = ☐ inches

1 yard = ☐ feet

1 yard = ☐ inches

1 meter = ☐ centimeters

Color the problems that match the number in the star.

  90

  100

  110

3 × 30	5 × 20	11 × 10
2 × 45	3 × 40	2 × 65
4 × 20	2 × 50	2 × 55

Lesson Activities

A

$4 \times 7 = \boxed{}$ $4 \times 9 = \boxed{}$ $4 \times 8 = \boxed{}$

$8 \times 7 = \boxed{}$ $8 \times 9 = \boxed{}$ $8 \times 8 = \boxed{}$

B

Escape the Maze (×8)

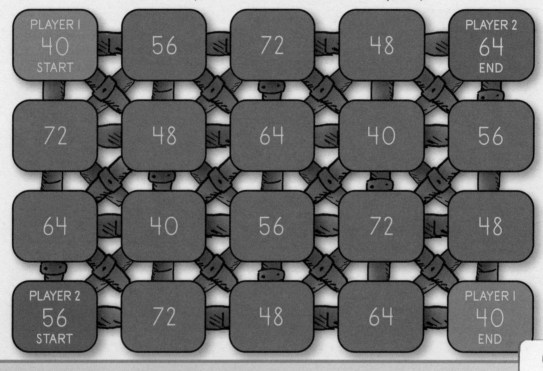

C

$4 \times 80 = \boxed{}$

$4 \times 8 \text{ tens} = \boxed{} \text{ tens}$

$5 \times 80 = \boxed{}$ $7 \times 60 = \boxed{}$ $9 \times 90 = \boxed{}$

$5 \times 8 \text{ tens} = \boxed{} \text{ tens}$ $7 \times 6 \text{ tens} = \boxed{} \text{ tens}$ $9 \times 9 \text{ tens} = \boxed{} \text{ tens}$

Practice

Complete.

×	4	8
×	5	8
×	2	8
×	6	8
×	8	8

×	3	8
×	9	8
×	10	8
×	7	8
×	1	8

Color the multiples in order from Start to End.

Multiples of 8

16	24	32	40	44
8	20	36	48	54
14	28	40	56	64
18	36	44	63	72
12	21	35	70	80

Start

END

Multiples of 7

7	14	21	28	35
12	16	54	49	42
24	48	64	56	60
45	36	40	63	70
35	30	32	72	80

Start

END

Color the problems that match the number in the star.

 540

| 9 × 60 |
| 9 × 50 |
| 9 × 70 |

 300

| 5 × 60 |
| 6 × 60 |
| 6 × 50 |

 480

| 6 × 90 |
| 6 × 80 |
| 6 × 70 |

 560

| 8 × 70 |
| 7 × 80 |
| 9 × 50 |

8.6

Review

Circle the fractions that equal one whole.
X the fractions that do not equal one whole.

$\frac{4}{4}$ $\frac{3}{4}$ $\frac{6}{6}$ $\frac{2}{3}$ $\frac{8}{8}$ $\frac{1}{2}$

$\frac{5}{8}$ $\frac{2}{2}$ $\frac{1}{4}$ $\frac{1}{8}$ $\frac{3}{6}$ $\frac{3}{3}$

Ethan made a pictograph about the cookies he baked.
Use the pictograph to answer the questions and complete the equations.

Cookies

Chocolate Chip	⊙ ⊙ ⊙ ⊙ ⊙
Oatmeal Raisin	⊙ ⊙ ⊙ ⊙ ⊙ ⊙ ⊙
Lemon	⊙ ⊙ ⊙ ⊙

⊙ = 8 cookies

How many chocolate chip cookies did he bake?

$$\boxed{} \times \boxed{} = \boxed{}$$

How many oatmeal raisin cookies did he bake?

$$\boxed{} \times \boxed{} = \boxed{}$$

How many lemon cookies did he bake?

$$\boxed{} \times \boxed{} = \boxed{}$$

Solve. Write the equation you use to solve the problem.

Sophia saved $64. Then, she earned $7 shoveling snow and spent $19 on a game.
How much money did she have left?

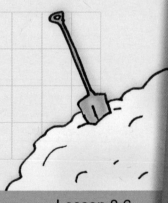

200   Lesson 8.6

Lesson Activities 👥

A

1 × 7 = ☐   6 × 7 = ☐

2 × 7 = ☐   7 × 7 = ☐

3 × 7 = ☐   8 × 7 = ☐

4 × 7 = ☐   9 × 7 = ☐

5 × 7 = ☐   10 × 7 = ☐

B

Multiplication Crash (×7)

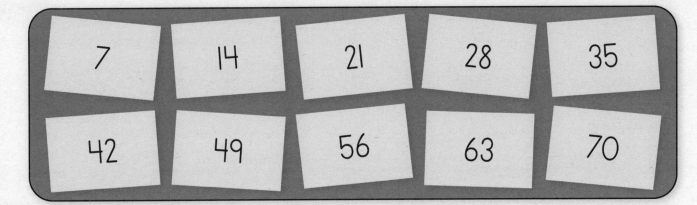

| 7 | 14 | 21 | 28 | 35 |
| 42 | 49 | 56 | 63 | 70 |

C

3 weeks = ☐ days

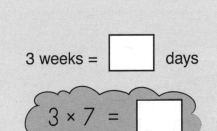

3 × 7 = ☐

5 weeks = ☐ days   4 weeks = ☐ days   7 weeks = ☐ days

Practice 👤 Complete.

	3
×	7

	2
×	7

	5
×	7

	6
×	7

	1
×	7

1	0
×	7

	9
×	7

	4
×	7

	8
×	7

	7
×	7

Complete.

2 weeks = [ ] days

6 weeks = [ ] days

10 weeks = [ ] days

9 weeks = [ ] days

Solve. Write a multiplication equation for each problem.

Mary Anne bought 7 packs of gum.
Each pack had 8 sticks.
How many sticks of gum did she buy?

Logan bought 8 packs of gum.
Each pack had 7 sticks.
How many sticks of gum did he buy?

[ ] × [ ] = [ ]

[ ] × [ ] = [ ]

Review **Round to the nearest dollar.**

$4.75	$3.99	$4.09	$0.99	$3.50	$3.70

Match pairs whose sum equals one whole.

$\frac{3}{4}$ $\frac{1}{6}$ $\frac{3}{8}$ $\frac{3}{6}$ $\frac{1}{8}$ $\frac{2}{3}$

$\frac{5}{8}$ $\frac{1}{4}$ $\frac{5}{6}$ $\frac{7}{8}$ $\frac{1}{3}$ $\frac{3}{6}$

Complete.

74 − 67 = ☐

71 − 67 = ☐

Start → 70 − 67 = ☐

★ 620 − 230 = ☐

620 − 30 = ☐

600 − 30 = ☐

★ 750 + 170 = ☐

750 + 70 = ☐

750 + 50 = ☐

7 × 60 = ☐

6 × 70 = ☐

6 × 7 = ☐

8.8

Lesson Activities 👥

A

×	6	7	8	9	10
5	30	35	40	45	50
6					60
7					70
8					80
9					90
10	60	70	80	90	100

B

3 weeks, 1 day = ☐ days

3 × 7 + 1 = ☐

2 weeks, 4 days = ☐ days

5 weeks, 2 days = ☐ days

4 weeks, 5 days = ☐ days

10 weeks, 6 days = ☐ days

Multiply and Add

			Score
☐ × ☐ + ☐			
☐ × ☐ + ☐			
☐ × ☐ + ☐			
☐ × ☐ + ☐			
☐ × ☐ + ☐			
Player 1 Total			

			Score
☐ × ☐ + ☐			
☐ × ☐ + ☐			
☐ × ☐ + ☐			
☐ × ☐ + ☐			
☐ × ☐ + ☐			
Player 2 Total			

Practice 👤   Complete.

$6 \times 6 =$ ☐ $9 \times 9 =$ ☐ $6 \times 8 =$ ☐

$5 \times 7 =$ ☐ $8 \times 8 =$ ☐ $7 \times 9 =$ ☐

$7 \times 7 =$ ☐ $7 \times 6 =$ ☐ $7 \times 4 =$ ☐

$9 \times 8 =$ ☐ $8 \times 7 =$ ☐ $9 \times 6 =$ ☐

Complete.

2 weeks, 1 day = ☐ days   3 weeks, 5 days = ☐ days

10 weeks, 3 days = ☐ days   7 weeks, 1 day = ☐ days

Review 👤 Complete.

- The pineapple costs 30¢ more than the bananas.

- The avocado costs $1.10 more than the bananas.

- The avocado costs $1.50 more than the celery.

$1.95

$

$

$

Complete the sequences.

Count by 12s

| 12 | | | | | | | 96 |

Count by 15s

| 15 | | | | | | | 120 |

Count by 20s

| | | 100 | | | | | |

Circle the fractions equivalent to ½. X the fractions that are not equivalent to ½.

 $\frac{2}{4}$ $\frac{3}{4}$ $\frac{4}{6}$ $\frac{5}{8}$ $\frac{2}{3}$ $\frac{3}{8}$

$\frac{1}{3}$ $\frac{2}{6}$ $\frac{3}{6}$ $\frac{7}{8}$ $\frac{4}{8}$ $\frac{6}{6}$

Unit Wrap-Up 👤 Color the multiples in order from Start to End.

Multiples of 6

8	10	14	56	60
6	12	15	48	54
21	18	25	42	45
20	24	30	36	40
25	27	32	52	39

Start (arrow points to 6) **END** (top right)

Multiples of 7

14	21	28	35	48
7	25	32	42	49
12	15	40	54	56
16	18	30	60	63
24	20	81	72	70

Start (arrow points to 7) **END** (bottom right)

Multiples of 8

8	16	24	32	40
14	12	36	56	48
27	44	54	64	72
15	25	45	70	80
20	21	50	49	100

Start (arrow points to 8) **END** (at 80)

Multiples of 9

24	30	32	35	80
18	27	36	40	90
9	12	45	48	81
15	20	54	63	72
21	25	56	70	64

Start (arrow points to 9) **END** (at 90)

Complete.

$6 \times 3 + 4 =$ ☐

$5 \times 8 + 3 =$ ☐

$10 \times 7 + 5 =$ ☐

$9 \times 4 + 2 =$ ☐

Match.

8×50		280
7×40		400
9×80		490
7×70		720

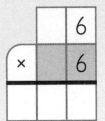

8.9

Unit Wrap-Up 👤 Complete.

	6			8			9			8			9
×	6		×	9		×	6		×	8		×	7

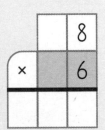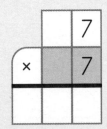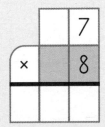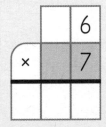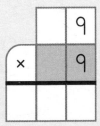

	8			7			7			6			9
×	6		×	7		×	8		×	7		×	9

Solve. Write the equations you use.

Spiders have 8 legs.
How many legs do 7 spiders have?

Katelyn earns $6 for washing the car.
If she washes the car 9 times, how much will she earn?

Liam's family is buying doughnuts for a party.
There are 8 doughnuts in each box.
They buy 3 boxes of plain doughnuts and 5 boxes of chocolate doughnuts.
How many doughnuts do they buy?

Kate's family is going on vacation in 5 weeks and 3 days.
How many days away is their trip?